Contents

THE BLISSFUL BHARAT

EXPLORING THE MOSAIC OF INDIA'S CULTURAL TAPESTRY

NITESH NIRUPAM

Republic of India

To the vibrant souls of **India**,

Whose stories, traditions, and colourful tapestry of cultures have inspired generations. You are the beating heart of this nation, and it is with immense gratitude and admiration that I dedicate this book to you. May your diverse traditions continue to enrich our lives and unite us in the celebration of our shared heritage.

With deepest appreciation,

Nitesh Nirupam

Foreword

India, with its myriad hues and endless depths, has always been a land of enchantment and wonder. In "The Blissful Bharat: Exploring the Mosaic of India's Cultural Tapestry" we embark on a journey through this timeless tapestry of cultures, where every thread tells a story and every shade whispers of centuries-old traditions.

As we turn the pages of this book, we are transported to a land where festivals light up the sky with bursts of colour and joy, where music and dance echo the rhythms of life, and where artistry and craftsmanship flourish in every corner. We encounter the warmth of hospitality, the richness of culinary delights, and the reverence for sacred spaces that embody the soul of India.

Through vivid narratives, stunning photographs, and insightful commentary, we come to understand the true essence of India's cultural heritage a kaleidoscope of traditions that celebrates unity in diversity. We witness the resilience of ancient customs in the face of modernity, and we marvel at the ingenuity of communities preserving their heritage for future generations.

But "The Blissful Bharat" is more than just a celebration of the past it is a call to embrace the present and shape the future. It reminds us that in the tapestry of human experience, every colour, every tradition, and every story has its place. It encourages us to cherish our differences and find strength in our shared humanity.

As we embark on this journey together, let us open our hearts to the beauty that surrounds us, let us embrace the diversity that defines us, and let us cherish the kaleidoscope of traditions that make India truly extraordinary.

Preface

Welcome to "The Blissful Bharat" a journey through the vibrant tapestry of India's cultural heritage. In this book, we invite you to explore the rich diversity and timeless traditions that define this remarkable nation. From the snow-capped peaks of the Himalayas to the sun-drenched shores of the Indian Ocean, India is a land of unparalleled beauty, where ancient customs and modern innovations coexist in harmony.

Each chapter of this book offers a glimpse into a different facet of India's cultural kaleidoscope, from its colourful festivals and intricate art forms to its diverse cuisines and sacred spaces. Through vivid descriptions, captivating stories, and stunning photographs, we aim to immerse you in the sights, sounds, and flavors of India, inviting you to experience the country's rich cultural heritage firsthand.

As you journey through these pages, you will discover the significance of traditions in Indian society, the rituals and symbolism behind major festivals, and the cultural origins of art forms such as painting, sculpture, and dance. You will embark on a culinary odyssey through the diverse cuisines of India, savoring the flavors of regional specialties and learning about the cultural significance of food in different communities.

You will also explore the world of traditional clothing and textiles, from vibrant sarees to intricately woven shawls, and delve into the architectural marvels of India's religious sites, including temples, mosques, churches, and gurdwaras. Through discussions on music, dance, language, literature, and traditional medicine, you will gain insight into the holistic approach to health and wellness that has sustained Indian culture for centuries.

Throughout this journey, we hope to convey the profound truth that lies at the heart of India's cultural heritage that amidst life's joys and sorrows, there is a divine presence that guides and sustains us, offering solace, hope, and eternal peace. It is a truth that transcends the boundaries of language, culture, and creed, reminding us of our shared humanity and the interconnectedness of all living beings in the vast tapestry of creation.

"The Blissful Bharat" is more than just a book it is an invitation to embark on a transformative journey of exploration, discovery, and appreciation for the rich tapestry of cultures that make India truly unique. So, come along and immerse yourself in the vibrant hues and timeless traditions of this extraordinary land. The journey awaits.

Acknowledgements

Writing a book is a journey that is not undertaken alone, and "The Blissful Bharat: Exploring the Mosaic of India's Cultural Tapestry" is no exception.

First and foremost, I extend my heartfelt thanks to the people of India, whose vibrant culture, rich traditions, and warm hospitality have inspired this book. Your stories, your customs, and your spirit are the beating heart of these pages.

I am immensely grateful to my family for their unwavering support, encouragement, and understanding throughout this journey. Your love and belief in me have been a constant source of strength and inspiration.

A special thank you to all the artisans, performers, and storytellers whose talent and dedication breathe life into the cultural tapestry of India. Your artistry and craftsmanship enrich our lives and remind us of the beauty of human creativity.

I would like to extend my appreciation to the team involved in the publication of this book.

Last but not least, I want to express my gratitude to the readers who embark on this journey with me. It is my sincere hope that "The Blissful Bharat " will inspire you, enlighten you, and deepen your appreciation for the kaleidoscope of traditions that make **India truly extraordinary.**

Prologue

In the heart of India, where the sun rises over ancient temples and sets behind bustling bazaars, lies a land of unparalleled beauty and diversity. This is a land where traditions are not merely preserved but celebrated with fervor and passion a land where every color tells a story, and every tradition is a thread in the rich tapestry of Indian culture.

In "The Blissful Bharat: Exploring the Mosaic of India's Cultural Tapestry" we embark on a journey through this enchanting realm, where the past meets the present, and where the echoes of centuries-old customs still resonate in the hearts of the people. From the snow-capped peaks of the Himalayas to the sun-kissed beaches of Kerala, each region of India offers a unique glimpse into the mosaic of its cultural heritage.

As we traverse the diverse landscapes and vibrant cityscapes of India, we encounter a kaleidoscope of traditions and festivals that light up the night sky with fireworks and fervor, music that stirs the soul, and dances that celebrate life's rhythms, art forms that reflect the beauty of nature and craftsmanship that honors ancestral wisdom.

But amidst the celebration and diversity, there is also a profound sense of unity a recognition that despite our differences, we are all part of the same intricate tapestry of humanity. It is this unity in diversity that defines the essence of India, and it is this spirit that we seek to cherish and celebrate in the pages of this book.

So come, dear reader, and join us on this journey through **The Blissful Bharat**. Let us immerse ourselves in the sights, sounds, and stories of this extraordinary land, and let us cherish the kaleidoscope of traditions that make India truly unique.

CHAPTER I

Introduction to India's Cultural Kaleidoscope

India, with its rich tapestry of culture, history, and geography, is truly a captivating country. It includes a diverse range of landscapes, from the majestic Himalayas in the north to the serene backwaters of Kerala in the south. India's diversity is not only reflected in its terrain but also in its people, traditions, and way of life.

At the heart of India's allure is its ability to seamlessly blend the ancient with the contemporary. Centuries-old traditions and customs are deeply ingrained in everyday life, coexisting harmoniously with the rapid pace of modernization and technological advancement. It's not uncommon to witness a traditional temple standing tall amidst a bustling metropolis adorned with skyscrapers or to see a group of people performing age-old rituals alongside the latest trends in fashion and entertainment.

One of the most striking aspects of India is its cultural mosaic, shaped by millennia of history and influenced by a multitude of civilizations, religions, and languages. Every region of India boasts its own unique cultural identity, manifested in its cuisine, music, dance, art, and festivals. From the vibrant colours of Rajasthan's folk dances to the serene chants of prayers in Varanasi, from the spicy flavors of street food in Mumbai to the intricate designs of Mughal architecture in Agra, India is a sensory feast that never fails to mesmerize.

But perhaps what truly sets India apart is its celebration of diversity. With over 1.3 billion people belonging to various ethnicities, religions, and linguistic groups, India is a melting pot of cultures where differences are not just tolerated but embraced. This diversity is not confined to its human population alone; India is also home to an astonishing variety of flora and fauna, with diverse ecosystems ranging from lush rainforests to arid deserts.

Yet, amidst this diversity, there is a common thread that unites the people of India - a sense of resilience, spirituality, and community. Despite facing numerous challenges, from poverty and inequality to environmental degradation and social unrest, Indians possess an indomitable spirit that has enabled them to overcome adversity time and again.

In essence, India is more than just a country; it's a living, breathing tapestry of humanity's collective heritage and aspirations. It's a place where ancient wisdom meets modern innovation, where the past informs the present, and where the possibilities for the future are as boundless as the horizons that stretch across its vast landscape.

As the sun begins its ascent, painting the sky with hues of pink and orange, India comes alive in a symphony of activity that is both chaotic and harmonious. In the bustling streets of Kolkata, the city's iconic yellow taxis weave through a maze of vendors selling their wares, while the aroma of spicy street food fills the air, tempting passersby with its irresistible allure. Here, amidst the hustle and bustle, one can witness the pulse of urban life, where centuries-old traditions collide with the rapid pace of modernization.

Meanwhile, in the tranquil backwaters of Kerala, a different scene unfolds. As dawn breaks, the still waters come alive with the gentle rhythm of oars slicing through the surface, guiding traditional wooden houseboats as they glide past verdant rice paddies and swaying coconut palms. The air is filled with the melodic chirping of birds and the occasional splash of a fish breaking the surface, creating a sense of serenity that is unparalleled.

India's diversity is on full display throughout the country, from the vibrant markets of Delhi to the remote villages of the Himalayas. In Rajasthan, the desert comes alive with the vibrant colours of traditional attire during festivals like Diwali and Holi, while in Tamil Nadu, the intricate carvings of ancient temples stand as a testament to the region's rich architectural heritage.

But it's not just the sights and sounds that make India come alive; it's also the warmth and hospitality of its people. Whether it's being welcomed into a stranger's home for a cup of *chai*, or being invited to join in a traditional dance during a village celebration, visitors to India are often struck by the genuine kindness and generosity of its inhabitants.

As the day progresses, India's vibrant energy only intensifies. In the bustling markets of Jaipur, the air is filled with the melodic sounds of vendors haggling over prices, while in Mumbai, the city's iconic *dabbawalas* weave through the streets, delivering home-cooked meals to thousands of office workers with remarkable precision.

As the sun begins to set, casting a warm glow over the landscape, India prepares for another night of festivities and celebration. From the colourful lights of Diwali illuminating the night sky to the rhythmic beats of a traditional *Kathak* performance, the country continues to dazzle and delight, leaving a lasting impression on all who have the privilege of experiencing its magic.

In the narrow lanes of Varanasi, where time seems to stand still, the spiritual heartbeat of India pulsates with an undeniable rhythm. As the first light of dawn breaks, pilgrims clad in vibrant hues of saffron and crimson descend upon the ancient *ghats* lining the sacred Ganges River. Here, amidst the labyrinthine alleys and narrow staircases that wind their way down to the water's edge, centuries-old rituals unfold with reverence and devotion.

Beneath the soft glow of the morning sun, devotees immerse themselves in the holy waters, their hands clasped in prayer as they seek purification and spiritual renewal. Along the *ghats*, priests clad in traditional attire perform elaborate ceremonies, their chants mingling with the gentle lapping of the river against the stone steps. Offerings of flowers, incense, and candles float downstream, carried by the currents of faith and tradition.

Meanwhile, in the pink-hued city of Jaipur, a different kind of magic unfolds amidst the opulent palaces and towering forts that dominate the skyline. Built centuries ago by the erstwhile rulers of Rajasthan, these architectural marvels stand as testaments to a bygone era of chivalry and grandeur. Inside the walls of the majestic Amber Fort, echoes of history reverberate through the ornately decorated halls and intricately carved chambers, transporting visitors back in time to an age of kings and queens.

As the day unfolds, the streets of Jaipur come alive with a kaleidoscope of colours and sounds. In the bustling bazaars of the old city, merchants peddle their wares, from handcrafted textiles and jewelry to fragrant spices and intricately embroidered fabrics. Here, amidst the hustle and bustle of everyday life, the spirit of Rajasthan shines through in every vibrant display and spirited exchange.

4

And yet, amidst the timeless rituals of Varanasi and the storied grandeur of Jaipur, there is a common thread that binds these disparate worlds together - a deep reverence for tradition, a profound connection to the land, and an unwavering sense of faith. In both cities, the past is not merely a relic of bygone days, but a living, breathing presence that continues to shape the present and inspire the future.

As the sun sets on another day in India, casting its golden glow over the landscape, the timeless allure of Varanasi and the regal splendor of Jaipur stand as reminders of the enduring beauty and complexity of this ancient land. And as night falls and the stars begin to twinkle overhead, the stories of pilgrims and kings, of rituals and royalty, continue to echo through the corridors of time, weaving a rich tapestry of history and heritage that is uniquely Indian.

Amidst the grandeur of its ancient cities and the chaotic energy of its bustling streets, India's greatest strength lies in its remarkable diversity, which serves as a unifying force that transcends regional, linguistic, and religious boundaries. With over 1.3 billion people belonging to a multitude of ethnicities, languages, and religions, India stands as a testament to the power of unity in diversity.

In the narrow lanes of Varanasi and the vibrant markets of Jaipur, this diversity is on full display, weaving a rich tapestry of cultures, traditions, and beliefs that coexist harmoniously. Here, amidst the timeless rituals of Varanasi's ghats and the regal splendor of Jaipur's palaces, people from all walks of life come together to celebrate their shared heritage and forge bonds of friendship and camaraderie.

Despite the myriad differences that exist among its people, India's ethos is rooted in the belief that diversity is not just a fact of life, but a source of strength and resilience. Throughout its long and storied history, India has been shaped by waves of migration, conquest, and trade, each contributing to the rich tapestry of cultures and traditions that define the nation today.

From the snowy peaks of the Himalayas to the sun-kissed shores of the Indian Ocean, India's landscapes are as diverse as its people, offering a glimpse into the vast array of ecosystems and climates that exist within its borders. This geographical diversity includes towering mountain ranges, lush forests, expansive deserts, fertile plains, and extensive coastlines, each contributing to the country's rich natural heritage. And yet, amidst this geographical diversity, there is a sense of unity that binds the nation together, transcending differences of language, religion, and ethnicity.

The northern region of India is dominated by the majestic Himalayas, which not only serve as a natural barrier but also as a source of numerous rivers that sustain millions of lives. The Himalayas are home to diverse flora and fauna and are revered in Indian culture and mythology. The region's cultural practices, from traditional dances to architectural styles, are influenced by the rugged, majestic terrain.

Moving southwards, the Indo-Gangetic Plain, one of the most fertile regions in the world, stretches across the northern part of India. This area, with its rich alluvial soil, supports extensive agricultural activities, forming the backbone of India's agrarian economy. The plains are dotted with bustling cities and historic sites, reflecting the historical and cultural amalgamation over centuries. The diversity of crops and agricultural practices across this region mirrors the diversity of its inhabitants, who speak different languages and follow various traditions but share a common reliance on the land.

Further west lies the Thar Desert, a stark contrast to the lush plains. The desert's arid landscape is home to resilient communities that have adapted to the harsh conditions. The culture here is vibrant, with colourful attire, folk music, and dance forms that have evolved to suit the desert environment. Despite the harsh living conditions, the spirit of hospitality and the sense of community is strong, showcasing how geographical challenges are overcome by social cohesion.

The central and eastern regions of India are characterized by dense forests and rich mineral resources. The dense jungles of the Deccan Plateau and the Eastern Ghats are biodiversity hotspots, sheltering a wide array of wildlife. These areas are inhabited by numerous indigenous tribes who have preserved their distinct cultures and ways of life for centuries. The tribal communities, with their unique languages, customs, and traditional knowledge of the forests, contribute to the cultural mosaic of India, emphasizing the coexistence of modernity and tradition.

As one moves towards the coastal regions, the Western and Eastern Ghats create a lush, tropical environment, supporting rich biodiversity and some of the most productive agricultural lands. The coastal plains are home to extensive plantations of spices, tea, coffee, and rice paddies. The coastal cities, such as Mumbai, Chennai, and Kolkata, are vibrant metropolises where the ancient and the modern intermingle seamlessly. These port cities have historically been gateways for trade and cultural exchange, bringing in influences from across the world and adding layers to the cultural fabric of India.

The southernmost part of India, the peninsular region, is surrounded by the Arabian Sea, the Indian Ocean, and the Bay of Bengal. This region enjoys a maritime climate and is famous for its backwaters, beaches, and unique ecosystems like the Sundarbans mangroves. The coastal culture is heavily influenced by the sea, with fishing communities and maritime trade playing a significant role in the economy and lifestyle. Festivals, cuisine, and daily life in these regions reflect a harmonious blend of local traditions and external influences, fostering a sense of unity despite geographical separations.

Throughout India, from the bustling urban centers to the tranquil rural villages, there is a common thread of unity that transcends the physical diversity of the land. This unity is deeply rooted in the shared values of family, community, and spirituality. Religious tolerance and respect for different ways of life are hallmarks of Indian society, creating a harmonious coexistence among its people. Festivals such as Diwali, Eid, Christmas, and Pongal are celebrated with equal fervor across the country, bringing together people from different backgrounds in a collective expression of joy and solidarity.

Language, too, serves as both a marker of diversity and a bridge of unity. India's linguistic diversity is vast, with hundreds of languages and dialects spoken across the country. The Constitution of India recognizes 22 official languages, but Hindi and English often serve as link languages, facilitating communication and unity among diverse linguistic communities.

In essence, India's geographical diversity, from its towering mountains to its expansive coastlines, is a testament to its natural wealth and cultural plurality. Yet, amidst this diversity, the sense of unity is palpable, driven by shared values, mutual respect, and a collective identity that transcends regional, linguistic, and religious differences. This unity in diversity is not just a slogan but a lived reality, shaping the nation's character and ensuring its strength and resilience.

Whether it's the joyous celebrations of Diwali that light up the night sky or the solemn prayers offered at mosques, temples, and *gurudwaras* across the country, India's cultural tapestry is a testament to the enduring spirit of unity that has sustained it through centuries of change and upheaval.

As the first rays of sunlight illuminate the landscape, casting a golden glow over the land, India awakens to another day filled with promise and possibility. And amidst the grandeur and the chaos, there is a sense of unity that prevails, reminding its people that, despite their differences, they are bound together by a common thread of shared history, shared aspirations, and a shared vision for the future.

Step foot into India, and you step into a world where every corner tells a story, where every festival is a celebration of life itself. From the colourful festivities of Diwali, where the night sky is lit up with a thousand *diyas*, to the joyous revelry of Holi, where streets are transformed into a riot of colours, India's festivals are a testament to the spirit of resilience and community that defines the country.

At the heart of India's cultural kaleidoscope lie its traditions – ancient customs and rituals that have been passed down from generation to generation. Whether it's the graceful movements of classical dance forms like *Bharatanatyam* and *Kathak* or the soul-stirring melodies of *Hindustani* and *Carnatic* music, traditions form the bedrock of Indian society, providing a sense of continuity and belonging in an ever-changing world.

But traditions are not static; they evolve and adapt with the times, reflecting the dynamic nature of Indian culture. Take, for example, the centuries-old tradition of Indian textiles, where handloom weavers create intricate patterns and designs that are a testament to their skill and craftsmanship. Today, these traditional techniques are being revived and reinvented by a new generation of designers who are breathing new life into this ancient art form.

Similarly, the age-old practice of *Ayurveda*, India's traditional system of medicine, is experiencing a resurgence as people seek alternative remedies to combat the stresses and strains of modern life. From yoga retreats in the Himalayas to *Ayurvedic* spas in Kerala, India's ancient healing traditions are attracting visitors from around the world who are eager to experience the rejuvenating powers of these age-old practices.

As the sun sets on another day in India, casting a warm, golden glow over the vast and varied landscapes, it signals not just the end of a day but the promise of a new dawn. In this land of ancient traditions and modern dynamism, every sunset is a reminder of the countless stories woven into the fabric of its existence. From the snow-capped peaks of the Himalayas to the serene backwaters of Kerala, from the bustling metropolises like Mumbai and Delhi to the tranquil villages in Rajasthan and Gujarat, India's diversity is both a marvel and a source of profound inspiration.

In the bustling streets, the air is filled with the symphony of life, vendors calling out their wares, the rhythmic clinking of *rickshaw* bells, the laughter of children, and the harmonious blend of multiple languages spoken in a single breath. Each face in the crowd tells a different story, shaped by a unique history, culture, and tradition. Here, the past and the present coexist in a vibrant dance, with ancient temples standing tall amidst skyscrapers, and traditional festivals celebrated with as much fervor as modern-day achievements.

India's diversity is its strength. Every encounter here is an opportunity to learn and grow. The myriad of festivals celebrated across the country, each with its rituals, cuisine, and customs, provide a glimpse into the country's rich cultural heritage. Whether it's the colourful exuberance of *Holi*, the lights and diyas of Diwali, the spiritual devotion of Eid, or the joyous celebrations of Christmas, each festival is a testament to India's inclusive spirit and its ability to celebrate differences with unity and harmony.

For the curious traveler, India is a never-ending journey of discovery. The majestic palaces of Rajasthan speak of a regal past, while the tranquil *ghats* of Varanasi whisper secrets of spirituality and enlightenment. The bustling markets of Hyderabad offer a sensory overload of colours, smells, and sounds, while the serene beaches of Goa provide a respite from the chaos of everyday life. Each region has its own unique charm, from the lush tea gardens of Assam to the vibrant textiles of Gujarat, from the classical dance forms of Tamil Nadu to the innovative technology hubs of Bangalore.

In the heart of this cultural kaleidoscope lies the essence of India, the people. Their resilience, warmth, and hospitality are unparalleled. It is in the small gestures of kindness, the sharing of a meal, and the exchange of stories, that one truly understands the soul of India. It is a place where strangers become friends, where every conversation is an opportunity to connect, and where every shared experience enriches the journey.

As the journey through India's cultural kaleidoscope continues, one realizes that the wonders of this land are endless. The ancient wisdom of its sages, the artistic brilliance of its craftsmen, and the scientific innovations of its youth—all converge to create a nation that is ever-evolving, yet deeply rooted in its traditions. For those who dare to explore, India offers not just a travel experience but a transformation, a chance to see the world through a different lens and to be forever changed by its beauty and complexity.

So, as the sun sets, casting its final glow over this incredible land, the promise of discoveries and endless possibilities fills the air. In India, every ending is but a new beginning and every moment is a step towards a future filled with hope and optimism.

CHAPTER II

The Vibrant Festivals of India

In India, festivals are not just events marked on calendars; they are ingrained in the very fabric of society, shaping traditions, fostering community bonds, and celebrating the rich tapestry of culture that defines the nation. From the snow-capped mountains of the north to the sun-kissed beaches of the south, each region boasts its calendar of festivals, each with its unique customs, rituals, and significance.

In the north, nestled among the towering peaks of the Himalayas, festivals like *Diwali*, *Holi*, and *Navratri* hold sway, filling the crisp mountain air with the scent of incense and the echoes of devotional songs. Diwali, the festival of lights, illuminates the darkness with flickering lamps and fireworks, symbolizing the triumph of light over darkness, good over evil. Meanwhile, Holi, the festival of colours, transforms the landscape into a riot of vibrant hues, as people of all ages come together to play, laugh, and forgive.

Traveling southwards, the landscape shifts, but the spirit of celebration remains undiminished. In Kerala, the land of backwaters and coconut groves, festivals like *Onam* and *Vishu* bring communities together in joyous celebration. *Onam*, the harvest festival, is marked by feasting, music, and the iconic snake boat races that draw spectators from far and wide. *Vishu*, on the other hand, heralds the New Year with rituals of prosperity and abundance, as families gather to exchange gifts and offerings.

In the heart of India, amidst the bustling cities and verdant plains of states like Madhya Pradesh and Uttar Pradesh, festivals like *Ganesh Chaturthi* and *Janmashtami* take center stage. *Ganesh Chaturthi,* dedicated to the beloved elephant-headed god *Ganesh*, sees elaborate processions and colourful idols adorning makeshift temples across the streets. Janmashtami, celebrating the birth of Lord *Krishna*, is marked by devotional songs, dance performances, and midnight prayers, as devotees reenact scenes from the life of the divine child.

In the coastal regions of the west and east, from the pink city of Jaipur to the temples of Tamil Nadu, festivals like Eid, Christmas, and Pongal unite people of diverse faiths and backgrounds in a spirit of harmony and goodwill. Eid, the festival of sacrifice, is a time for feasting and charity, as Muslims come together to commemorate the end of *Ramadan.* Christmas celebrated with fervor and joy, brings communities together in prayer, song, and acts of kindness, as churches and homes are adorned with lights and decorations. *Pongal,* the harvest festival of Tamil Nadu, is a time of thanksgiving and abundance, as families gather to cook traditional dishes, exchange gifts, and pay homage to the sun god.

In every corner of India, from the bustling metropolises to the remote villages, festivals serve as anchors of cultural identity, reinforcing values of unity, diversity, and resilience. Through their rituals and celebrations, they connect people to their roots, forge bonds of friendship and kinship, and inspire a sense of belonging that transcends boundaries of caste, creed, and language. Indeed, in the vibrant tapestry of India's cultural landscape, festivals are not just moments in time; they are timeless expressions of the indomitable spirit of its people.

Let's start our journey with *Diwali*, the festival of lights, celebrated with great fervor and enthusiasm across the country. *Diwali*, also known as *Deepavali*, holds immense significance in Hindu culture, symbolizing the victory of light over darkness and good over evil. As the night sky is illuminated with a dazzling display of fireworks and lamps, families come together to exchange gifts, share sweets, and offer prayers to the goddess *Lakshmi* for prosperity and good fortune. From the lighting of earthen lamps (*diyas*) to the creation of intricate *rangoli* designs, *Diwali* is a time of joyous celebration and spiritual renewal.

In the days leading up to *Diwali*, homes, and streets across India are transformed into glittering spectacles of light and colour, marking one of the most vibrant and eagerly awaited festivals of the year. The preparations for *Diwali* begin well in advance, as families and communities come together to welcome the festival of lights with enthusiasm and devotion.

People meticulously clean and decorate their homes, a practice rooted in the belief that a clean and beautiful house will invite the blessings of *Lakshmi*, the goddess of wealth and prosperity. This ritual cleaning, known as 'Diwali cleaning,' is seen as an opportunity to purge the household of any negative energy and to create a welcoming environment for the divine. From sweeping and dusting to more intensive tasks like painting and renovating, the entire household is involved in ensuring that every nook and cranny is spotless.

As the cleaning progresses, homes are adorned with vibrant decorations. *Rangoli*, intricate patterns created using coloured powders, rice, or flower petals, are designed at the entrances of homes to welcome guests and deities alike. These artistic creations, often depicting geometric shapes, flowers, and religious symbols, add a splash of colour and creativity to the festive ambiance. *Rangoli*, a traditional art form, adds to the festive spirit. These intricate designs, created using coloured powders, rice, and flower petals, adorn doorsteps and floors, serving both as decoration and as a way to welcome guests and deities into the home. Each rangoli pattern, unique and vibrant, is a manifestation of the creativity and cultural heritage passed down through generations. Doors and windows are decorated with strings of marigold flowers and mango leaves, believed to bring good fortune.

Illumination is a key element of *Diwali*, symbolizing the victory of light over darkness and knowledge over ignorance. Homes and streets are adorned with rows of oil lamps, known as diyas, as well as electric lights and candles. *Diyas* are placed in windows, doorways, and along pathways, creating a warm, inviting glow. The sight of countless tiny flames flickering against the night sky is truly magical, filling the air with a sense of peace and harmony.

The atmosphere is charged with anticipation and excitement as the markets become bustling hubs of activity. Streets and *bazaars* are lined with stalls selling an array of goods, from traditional clay lamps and decorations to the latest in fashion and technology. People throng these markets to buy new clothes, which are traditionally worn during the festival as a symbol of new beginnings and fresh starts. Garments range from traditional attire such as *sarees* and *kurta-pajamas* to contemporary styles, catering to all tastes and preferences.

On the evening of *Diwali*, families gather to perform the *Lakshmi Puja*, a ritual to honor the goddess. This ritual typically involves placing idols or pictures of *Lakshmi* and

Ganesha on a beautifully adorned *altar*, surrounded by offerings of flowers, fruits, sweets, and coins. The family then recites prayers and mantras, seeking blessings for health, wealth, and happiness in the coming year.

As dusk falls, the true magic of *Diwali* unfolds. The flicker of countless *diyas* (earthen lamps) illuminates homes, temples, and public spaces, creating a warm, golden glow that symbolizes the dispelling of ignorance and the embrace of wisdom. These lamps, often placed in rows on windowsills, balconies, and courtyards, are a tribute to the return of Lord *Rama* to his kingdom of Ayodhya after a 14-year exile, as described in *Ramayana*.

Gift-giving is an integral part of *Diwali* celebrations, reflecting the spirit of sharing and goodwill. Throughout the evening, the exchange of gifts and sweets fosters a sense of community and goodwill. Shoppers can be seen selecting gifts for family and friends, with popular choices including sweets, dry fruits, jewelry, and gadgets. Sweets, or *mithai*, hold a special place in Diwali festivities. Shops overflow with a variety of confections like *ladoos*, *barfis*, and *jalebis*, each more tempting than the last. These sweets are not only enjoyed within the family but are also exchanged as gifts, symbolizing the sweetness and joy of the occasion.

In the days leading up to *Diwali*, special markets known as '*Diwali Melas* ' spring up in many cities and towns. These fairs offer a delightful mix of shopping, entertainment, and food. Stalls selling handcrafted items, traditional toys, and festive decorations draw crowds, while stages set up for cultural performances feature traditional dances, music, and theatrical presentations. These melas provide a vibrant, communal space where people can immerse themselves in the festive spirit.

As the day of *Diwali* approaches, the excitement reaches a crescendo. Families prepare elaborate feasts, with each region boasting its own set of traditional dishes. Kitchens are filled with the aroma of rich curries, fragrant rice dishes, and delectable sweets being prepared. The culinary preparations are often a collaborative effort, bringing together multiple generations to cook and share family recipes.

On the night of *Diwali*, the celebrations culminate in a grand display of fireworks. The skies are lit up with a dazzling array of colours and patterns, as people of all ages gather to watch and participate in the spectacle. The sound of firecrackers and the sight of fireworks create an exhilarating atmosphere, symbolizing the joy and exuberance of the festival. The night sky comes alive with the brilliance of fireworks, as bursts of colour and sound fill the air. This spectacle is not just for entertainment but also has symbolic meanings. Fireworks are believed to ward off evil spirits and add to the jubilant atmosphere, their dazzling displays mirroring the inner joy and the light within every heart.

The days leading up to *Diwali* are marked by a flurry of activities that transform homes and streets into radiant displays of light and colour. The meticulous cleaning and decorating of homes, the bustling markets filled with shoppers, and the shared anticipation of the festivities all contribute to the unique and enchanting atmosphere of *Diwali*. It is a time of renewal, celebration, and communal harmony, reflecting the deep cultural and spiritual significance of this beloved festival.

In the midst of all the festivities, *Diwali* also serves as a profound time for introspection and renewal. This aspect of the festival, though quieter than the outward celebrations, is deeply significant and adds a layer of spiritual depth to the occasion. *Diwali*, the festival of lights, symbolizes the triumph of light over darkness and good over evil, prompting individuals to turn inward and reflect on their own lives.

The process of introspection during *Diwali* encourages people to take stock of their journeys. It is a time to contemplate past actions, recognize mistakes, and seek ways to improve. This period of reflection often leads to a reassessment of one's goals and aspirations, inspiring a renewed sense of purpose and direction. The symbolic lighting of *diyas* (oil lamps) represents dispelling the darkness within, fostering an environment conducive to personal growth and spiritual awakening.

Letting go of past grievances is another essential aspect of *Diwali's* introspective spirit. The festival encourages individuals to release feelings of anger, resentment, and bitterness that may have accumulated over time. By doing so, they create space for positive emotions and experiences. This act of letting go is not only emotionally liberating but also strengthens mental resilience, enabling people to face future challenges with a clearer and more positive mindset.

This Festival also marks a time to look forward to new beginnings with hope and positivity. The preparation and celebration of the festival itself embody renewal and rejuvenation. Just as homes are cleaned and decorated, individuals strive to cleanse their hearts and minds of negativity, making way for fresh opportunities and brighter prospects. This sense of renewal is reflected in the tradition of wearing new clothes and exchanging gifts, symbolizing a fresh start and the joy of giving and receiving.

Rekindling relationships is a fundamental part of the *Diwali* celebration. The festival provides an opportunity to reconnect with family, friends, and loved ones. It is a time to strengthen bonds that may have weakened over the year due to busy schedules and life's demands. Visiting relatives, sharing meals, and exchanging heartfelt gifts are common practices that help reinforce these relationships. The communal aspect of *Diwali* fosters a sense of belonging and togetherness, reminding people of the importance of their social connections.

Forgiveness and reconciliation are key themes during *Diwali*. The festival encourages individuals to forgive past wrongs and mend strained relationships. By extending forgiveness, both the giver and the receiver experience a sense of relief and healing. This act of reconciliation can pave the way for healthier and more harmonious interactions in the future. The tradition of visiting and greeting neighbors and friends during *Diwali* embodies this spirit of goodwill and mutual respect.

Extending a hand of friendship and love to those around is another integral part of *Diwali's* ethos. The festival promotes inclusivity and generosity, urging people to reach out to others, including those who may be less fortunate. Acts of charity and kindness are encouraged, such as distributing food, clothes, and other essentials to those in need. These gestures of compassion and empathy help to build a more caring and cohesive society.

In essence, *Diwali* is more than just a festival; it's a celebration of life's triumphs and an affirmation of the human spirit's capacity for joy, generosity, and growth. It brings together the old and the young, the rich and the poor, transcending barriers and creating a sense of unity and harmony across the vast and diverse landscape of

India.

Next, we have *Holi*, the festival of colours, where people of all ages come together to play with coloured powders popularly known as *Gulal* and water, celebrating the triumph of good over evil. With laughter and merriment echoing through the streets, *Holi* is a time for forgiveness and renewal, a celebration of the bonds of friendship and community. Holi is associated with various legends, including the story of *Prahlad* and *Holika* and the love of *Radha* and *Krishna*. Today, Holi transcends religious boundaries and is celebrated by people of all faiths and backgrounds as a joyous festival of love and unity.

The preparations for Holi begin days in advance with the collection of wood and other combustible materials for the *Holika Dahan*, a significant ritual that takes place on the eve of *Holi*. This ritual involves lighting bonfires to symbolize the burning of the demoness *Holika*, who was defeated by the unwavering devotion and faith of *Prahlad*. According to the legend, *Holika*, who had a boon that made her immune to fire, attempted to kill her nephew *Prahlad* on behalf of his evil father, King *Hiranyakashipu*. However, due to *Prahlad's* devout faith in Lord *Vishnu*, *Holika's* boon failed, and she was consumed by the flames while *Prahlad* emerged unharmed. This story underscores the festival's theme of the triumph of good over evil and the power of faith.

On the day of *Holi*, the atmosphere is charged with excitement and joy. Streets, parks, and open spaces become vibrant arenas where people gather to drench each other in a riot of colours. The air is filled with the playful shouts of children and adults alike, as they smear each other with *gulal* (coloured powder) and spray coloured water using *pichkaris* (water guns) and water balloons. The exuberance of the celebration is palpable, with everyone joining in the fun, regardless of age, status, or social barriers.

Holi is also a time for music and dance. Traditional folk songs, known as *Holi* songs, are sung, and people dance to the rhythmic beats of drums (*dhols*) and other musical instruments. In some regions, special performances like the *Matki Phod* (breaking the pot) reenact the playful antics of Lord *Krishna*, who, according to legend, loved to steal butter and play pranks on the village girls (*gopis*) with his friends.

The festival is also synonymous with delicious food and sweets. Special delicacies such as *gujiya* (sweet dumplings filled with a mixture of *mawa* and dried fruits), *malpua* (a type of pancake soaked in sugar syrup), and *bhang thandai* (a traditional drink made with milk, spices, and cannabis) are prepared and shared among family and friends. The sharing of food not only enhances the festive spirit but also reinforces the sense of community and togetherness.

Holi is a time for reconciliation and the mending of broken relationships. It is customary for people to visit friends and family, applying colours to each other's faces and exchanging warm greetings and sweets. This gesture of goodwill fosters a sense of unity and harmony, dissolving past grievances and misunderstandings. The playful nature of the festival encourages people to let go of their inhibitions and embrace the joy and spontaneity of the moment.

In many parts of India, *Holi* celebrations extend beyond the day itself, with festivities continuing for several days. Each region adds its unique touch to the celebrations. In Vrindavan and Mathura, where Lord *Krishna* spent his childhood, *Holi* is celebrated with unparalleled fervor. The

Lathmar Holi of Barsana, where women playfully beat men with sticks, and the *Phoolon ki Holi* of Vrindavan, where flowers are used instead of colours, are just a few examples of the diverse ways in which the festival is celebrated.

Holi's inclusive nature has helped it transcend religious and cultural boundaries, making it a festival celebrated by people of all faiths and backgrounds. Its message of love, unity, and the triumph of good over evil resonates universally, making *Holi* not just a celebration of colours, but a celebration of life itself.

In conclusion, *Holi* is a vibrant and joyous festival that brings people together in a colourful celebration of unity, love, and renewal. It is a time when differences are set aside, and the shared human spirit of joy and community is celebrated with exuberance and warmth. Whether through the playful throwing of colours, the sharing of festive foods, or the singing and dancing that fills the streets, *Holi* is a reminder of the beauty of life and the bonds that connect us all.

Moving on to Eid, the festival of sacrifice, celebrated by Muslims around the world to commemorate the willingness of Ibrahim (Abraham) to sacrifice his son as an act of obedience to God. Eid al-Fitr, which marks the end of Ramadan, the Islamic holy month of fasting, and Eid al-Adha, which commemorates Ibrahim's willingness to sacrifice his son, are the two main festivals celebrated by Muslims in India. From early morning prayers at the mosque to feasting delicious delicacies with family and friends, Eid is a time of reflection, gratitude, and generosity. It is a time for Muslims to come together in prayer and celebration, reaffirming their faith and strengthening their bonds of brotherhood and sisterhood.

Finally, we have Christmas, celebrated by Christians across India with great pomp and splendor. From decorating Christmas trees and exchanging gifts to attending midnight mass and singing carols, Christmas is a time for joy, love, and compassion, a celebration of the birth of Jesus Christ and the spirit of giving. In India, Christmas is celebrated with a unique blend of traditional customs and local traditions, reflecting the country's diverse cultural heritage. From the bustling markets of Kolkata to the serene churches of Goa, Christmas brings people together in a spirit of warmth and goodwill, transcending religious and cultural boundaries.

India's festivals are a testament to its extraordinary regional diversity, each one reflecting the unique cultural heritage and traditions of different parts of the country. These celebrations, imbued with local flavors and customs, create a vibrant mosaic that defines the nation's cultural landscape. Let's delve deeper into some of these region-specific festivals that illustrate the richness and diversity of India's traditions.

- **Baisakhi in Punjab**

    In the northern state of Punjab, the festival of *Baisakhi* is celebrated with great enthusiasm and joy, embodying both agrarian and spiritual significance. *Baisakhi* marks the harvest of the Rabi crop, making it one of the most important festivals for *Punjabi* farmers who celebrate the bounty of their hard work. It also commemorates the formation of the *Khalsa* in 1699 by *Guru Gobind Singh*, a pivotal event in *Sikh* history that established the community of baptized *Sikhs*.

    The celebrations of *Baisakhi* begin early in the morning as people dress in their finest traditional attire, often featuring bright and vibrant colours that reflect the joy and festivity of the occasion. Men typically wear kurta-pajamas with colourful turbans, while women wear *salwar-kameez* or lehengas adorned with intricate embroidery and jewelry. The day starts with families gathering in *gurudwaras* (Sikh temples) to offer prayers and gratitude for the harvest. These prayers are followed by *kirtans* (devotional singing), where the air is filled with the melodious recitation of hymns from the *Guru Granth Sahib,* the holy scripture of Sikhism.

The atmosphere inside the gurdwaras is one of devotion and reverence. After the prayers and kirtans, the community partakes in the *langar*, a communal meal served to all, regardless of caste, creed, or status. This tradition of sharing a meal emphasizes equality and community spirit, core principles of Sikhism.

As the day progresses, the streets come alive with vibrant processions known as *Nagar Kirtans.* These processions are a key highlight of the *Baisakhi* celebrations. Devotees, both young and old, walk together, chanting hymns and spreading messages of peace and unity. The processions are led by the revered *Guru Granth Sahib*, carried on a beautifully decorated float, followed by groups of devotees singing and performing. The rhythmic beats of *dhols* (drums) and the sounds of joyous singing fill the air, creating an infectious energy that draws in even the bystanders.

A notable feature of these processions is the display of *Gatka*, a traditional Sikh martial art. Skilled practitioners, often dressed in traditional warrior attire, perform breathtaking feats of swordsmanship and other martial techniques. These displays not only showcase physical prowess but also pay homage to the martial traditions of the Sikh community, reminding onlookers of the historical and cultural significance of *Baisakhi*.

One of the most anticipated aspects of *Baisakhi* is the traditional dance forms of *Bhangra* and *Giddha*. *Bhangra*, originally a harvest dance, is performed by men who wear colourful *kurtas* and *lungis*, accessorized with vibrant turbans. The dance is characterized by energetic and exuberant movements, including high jumps, kicks, and synchronized claps, all performed to the lively beats of the dhol. *Giddha*, performed by women, is equally spirited, featuring graceful yet vigorous movements. The women, dressed in brightly coloured *salwar-kameez* and adorned with traditional jewelry, sing *boliyan* (folk couplets) while performing intricate dance steps. These dances are not just a form of entertainment but also a way of expressing the collective joy and gratitude of the community for the bountiful harvest.

In addition to the prayers, processions, and dances, *Baisakhi* is also marked by vibrant fairs. These fairs are bustling with activity and offer a wide array of attractions. Stalls selling traditional Punjabi food, such as *makki di roti* and *sarson da saag, jalebi*, and *lassi*, draw large crowds. Folk music performances and traditional games like tug-of-war, wrestling, and *kabaddi* add to the festive spirit. Artisans display their crafts, and people engage in buying and selling local handicrafts and agricultural products.

The communal aspect of *Baisakhi* is further highlighted by the sense of togetherness and collective celebration that permeates the festivities. Families and friends come together, sharing meals, participating in various activities, and enjoying the lively atmosphere. The festival fosters a strong sense of community, reinforcing social bonds and promoting a spirit of unity and solidarity.

In essence, *Baisakhi* is a festival that beautifully intertwines religious devotion, cultural traditions, and communal harmony. It is a time when the people of Punjab, and *Sikhs* worldwide, come together to celebrate their heritage, express gratitude for the harvest, and renew their commitment to the values of their faith. The joyous celebrations, marked by prayers, music, dance, and communal feasting, make *Baisakhi* a vibrant and deeply meaningful festival, reflecting the rich cultural tapestry of Punjab.

- **Navratri in Gujarat**

In the western state of Gujarat, *Navratri* is a festival that spans nine nights and is dedicated to the worship of the goddess *Durga*. This vibrant and deeply spiritual festival is celebrated with immense fervor, blending devotion, cultural traditions, and a strong sense of community. *Navratri*, meaning "nine nights," honors the different forms of the goddess *Durga*, symbolizing the victory of good over evil and the celebration of feminine power.

Garba and *Dandiya Raas* are the focal points of *Navratri* celebrations, each offering a unique and dynamic expression of joy and devotion. *Garba* involves rhythmic, circular movements performed by women around a centrally placed lamp, called a *garbi*, or an image of the goddess. This dance symbolizes the cycle of life and the constant interplay of the human and the divine. The performers, often dressed in traditional *chaniya cholis* (embroidered, colourful skirts with matching blouses and dupattas), move gracefully in circles, clapping their hands and singing along to devotional songs. The lamp or image at the center represents Durga, the source of all energy, and the dancers' movements around it signify the continuous cycle of creation and destruction.

Dandiya Raas, on the other hand, is a lively and energetic dance performed with sticks (dandiyas) and typically involves pairs or groups. This dance mimics the mock fight between Durga and the demon *Mahishasura*, showcasing the triumph of good over evil. Participants strike their dandiyas together in rhythm, creating a captivating beat that resonates with the traditional and contemporary music played during the festival. Men and women both participate in *Dandiya Raas*, often dressed in traditional attire, with men wearing *kedias* (short, flared shirts) and *dhotis*. The synchronized movements, the vibrant clashing of sticks, and the infectious energy of the dancers create a mesmerizing spectacle.

The streets of Gujarat come alive during *Navratri* with brightly lit pavilions known as *pandals*. These pandals are often elaborately decorated with lights, flowers, and intricate designs, serving as the epicenter of the celebrations. People gather here in large numbers to dance, sing, and celebrate. The atmosphere is electric, filled with the sounds of traditional Gujarati music as well as contemporary tunes that inspire people to join in the dance. Each night of *Navratri*, the festivities continue late into the night, with participants tirelessly dancing in devotion and joy.

The festival of Navratri also includes various rituals and spiritual practices. Devotees observe fasting during the nine days, consuming only specific foods that are considered pure and appropriate for the occasion. This fasting is a form of penance and devotion, believed to purify the body and mind. Special prayers and pujas are performed daily to honor the different avatars of *Durga*. Each day is dedicated to a different manifestation of the goddess, and the rituals performed seek her blessings for health, prosperity, and protection.

In addition to fasting and prayers, other rituals include the setting up of a *Kalash* (a sacred pot) filled with water and topped with a coconut, surrounded by fresh mango leaves. This Kalash is worshipped throughout the nine days, symbolizing the presence of the goddess in the household. On the eighth or ninth day, known as *Ashtami* or *Navami*, young girls, considered to be the embodiment of the goddess, are invited to homes and served a special meal, a ritual known as *Kanya Puja*.

The colourful, embellished outfits worn by participants add to the festive atmosphere of *Navratri*. Women wear *chaniya cholis* adorned with mirror work, beads, and sequins, while men wear *kedias* with intricate embroidery. The vibrant costumes, along with traditional jewelry and accessories, create a visual feast, reflecting the rich cultural heritage of Gujarat.

Overall, *Navratri* in Gujarat is a celebration of life, devotion, and community spirit. It is a time when people come together to honor the goddess *Durga*, celebrate their cultural traditions, and experience the joy of dancing and singing. The festival's combination of spiritual practices, energetic dances, and communal gatherings makes it one of the most cherished and vibrant festivals in the state, embodying the spirit of Gujarat's rich cultural tapestry.

- **Bihu in Assam**

  In the northeastern state of Assam, *Bihu* stands as the principal festival, celebrated with great enthusiasm to mark the Assamese New Year and the onset of the harvest season. Observed three times a year – *Rongali* or *Bohag Bihu* in April, *Kongali* or *Kati Bihu* in October, and *Bhogali* or *Magh Bihu* in January – each celebration holds its unique significance, with *Rongali Bihu* being the most prominent and vibrant.

  Rongali Bihu, also known as *Bohag Bihu*, is the most significant of the three Bihu festivals, heralding the Assamese New Year and the arrival of spring. This festival is characterized by a time of feasting, dancing, and merriment, reflecting the joy of a new beginning and the anticipation of a fruitful harvest. The festivities last for several days and are marked by a series of traditional and cultural activities that bring communities together.

  One of the central features of *Rongali Bihu* is the performance of traditional folk dances, particularly the *Bihu* dance. Young men and women, dressed in their finest traditional attire, come together to perform these dances with great energy and enthusiasm. The traditional attire for women includes the *Mekhela Chador,* a two-piece garment made of silk or cotton, often in vibrant colours and adorned with intricate patterns. Men typically wear *dhotis* and *gamchas* (traditional handwoven towels). The dance movements are lively and rhythmic, often mimicking the daily activities of farmers in the fields, such as planting, sowing, and harvesting. This connection to agrarian life underscores the festival's roots in celebrating agricultural prosperity.

The sound of traditional musical instruments adds to the festive atmosphere. The *dhol* (drum), *Pepa* (a flute-like instrument made from buffalo horn), and *gcgona* (a reed instrument) create an infectious, celebratory ambiance. The rhythmic beats and melodies of these instruments are integral to the *Bihu* dance, providing a backdrop that encourages everyone to join in the revelry. The music and dance together encapsulate the spirit of *Rongali Bihu*, embodying joy, unity, and cultural pride.

Feasting is another crucial aspect of *Rongali Bihu*. Families come together to prepare and enjoy an array of traditional Assamese delicacies that are both sweet and savory. *Pitha*, a type of rice cake, is a staple during Bihu and comes in various forms, such as *til pitha* (made with sesame seeds) and *narikol pitha* (made with coconut). *Laru*, sweet balls made from coconut and sesame, is also popular. Additionally, a variety of savory dishes, including fish, meat, and vegetable preparations, are prepared and shared among family and friends. The act of cooking and sharing these traditional foods reinforces communal bonds and the spirit of hospitality that defines Assamese culture.

During *Rongali Bihu*, ceremonial lamps are lit, and prayers are offered to the deities to seek blessings for a bountiful harvest and prosperity in the coming year. These rituals reflect the deep spiritual connection that the festival maintains with agrarian life and the natural world. Temples and homes are adorned with flowers, and offerings are made to seek divine favor. This spiritual aspect of *Bihu* highlights the reverence for nature and the acknowledgment of its vital role in sustaining human life.

Kongali or *Kati Bihu*, celebrated in October, is a more somber occasion compared to *Rongali Bihu*. It coincides with the period when the fields are in the growth phase and the granaries are not yet full. During *Kati Bihu*, farmers light lamps in their fields and near their homes to ward off evil spirits and pests, praying for a good harvest. This festival is marked by simplicity and introspection, focusing on the well-being of the crops and the hope for future abundance.

Bhogali or *Magh Bihu*, celebrated in January, marks the end of the harvest season and is a time of feasting and merriment, much like *Rongali Bihu*. It is a celebration of the successful harvest and the abundance it brings. The night before *Bhogali Bihu*, known as *Uruka*, is celebrated with community feasts, bonfires, and traditional games. People gather to cook and share meals, strengthening communal ties and celebrating the fruits of their labor.

In summary, *Bihu* in Assam is not just a festival but a reflection of the region's agrarian lifestyle and cultural heritage. *Rongali Bihu,* with its vibrant dances, rhythmic music, and sumptuous feasts, epitomizes the joy and optimism of a new beginning. *Kongali Bihu*, with its rituals and prayers, underscores the hope and dedication of farmers. *Bhogali Bihu*, with its communal feasts and celebrations, marks the gratitude for a successful harvest. Together, these three Bihu festivals embody the cycle of agricultural life and the deep cultural and spiritual connection of the Assamese people to their land and traditions.

- **Onam in Kerala**

In the southern state of Kerala, *Onam* stands as the grandest and most vibrant festival, celebrated with immense pomp and splendor to honor the mythical King *Mahabali* and the harvest season. This ten-day festival, rich with cultural events, traditional games, and culinary delights, beautifully showcases the diverse and rich heritage of Kerala.

One of the most iconic aspects of *Onam* is the creation of *Pookalam*, intricate flower carpets laid out in front of homes to welcome King *Mahabali*. *Pookalam* designs start simple on the first day of the festival, known as *Atham*, and become increasingly elaborate as more flowers are added each day until the final day, *Thiruvonam*. The creation of these vibrant and complex floral designs is a communal activity, bringing families and communities together in a shared effort. The *Pookalam* not only serves as a visual treat but also symbolizes the warm hospitality and joy with which King *Mahabali* is welcomed back to the land he once ruled.

Traditional boat races, known as *Vallam Kali*, are another highlight of the *Onam* festival. These races feature long, narrow boats known as snake boats (*Chundan Vallam*), which are elaborately decorated and manned by up to a hundred rowers. The most famous of these races is the Nehru Trophy Boat Race held on the *Punnamada* Lake in Alappuzha. The sight of these majestic boats cutting through the water in perfect rhythm, accompanied by traditional boat songs, draws thousands of spectators, both locals and tourists. The boat races embody the spirit of teamwork and the competitive zeal that characterize the festival.

The festivities also include the grand *Onam Sadya*, a sumptuous feast served on banana leaves. This traditional meal comprises a variety of vegetarian dishes, each prepared meticulously and served in a specific order. Dishes include *avial* (a mixed vegetable curry with coconut), *sambar* (a lentil-based vegetable stew), *rasam* (a spicy-sour soup), and several types of *payasam* (sweet puddings made with milk, rice, and jaggery). *Onam Sadya* is not just a meal but a celebration of Kerala's culinary heritage and the spirit of sharing and togetherness. Families gather to enjoy this feast, reinforcing social bonds and the communal spirit of the festival.

Onam is also celebrated with traditional arts and performances that add to the festive atmosphere. *Kathakali*, a classical dance-drama known for its elaborate costumes, vibrant makeup, and expressive gestures, is performed during *Onam*. These performances often depict stories from Hindu epics, bringing to life the rich mythological heritage of Kerala. *Pulikali*, or the tiger dance, is another unique performance where men paint themselves like tigers and dance to the beats of traditional instruments. This lively and energetic dance is a crowd favorite, symbolizing the wild and untamed spirit of the festival.

The majestic elephant processions of *Thrissur Pooram* and the captivating *Kathakali* performances in *Kochi* are other highlights that showcase Kerala's cultural heritage to the world. *Thrissur Pooram*, although not part of *Onam*, shares a similar grandeur and involves the parading of beautifully decorated elephants accompanied by traditional percussion ensembles. These processions, with their pageantry and splendor, add to the festive atmosphere, highlighting the state's rich traditions.

Folk dances like *Thiruvathira Kali*, performed by women around a lamp, and *Kummattikali*, a colourful mask dance, are also integral to the *Onam* celebrations. These dances, along with other traditional performances, serve to keep Kerala's cultural heritage alive and thriving, providing a platform for artists to showcase their skills and for the community to celebrate their shared history.

In addition to these cultural performances, various traditional games and sports are organized during *Onam*. Competitions like tug-of-war, archery, and *Kabaddi* bring communities together in friendly competition, further enhancing the spirit of camaraderie and festivity.

Onam's rich tapestry of events, from the creation of *Pookalam* to the grand *Onam Sadya* and the vibrant boat races and cultural performances, reflects the deep-rooted traditions and communal harmony of Kerala. The festival is a time of joy, celebration, and gratitude, honoring the mythical King *Mahabali's* reign of prosperity and equality, and welcoming the harvest season with open hearts and joyous spirits. Through *Onam*, Kerala's cultural heritage is celebrated in all its glory, offering a glimpse into the state's traditions, values, and the enduring spirit of its people.

These regional festivals highlight the cultural diversity and unity of India, each one a unique celebration of the local heritage and traditions. They reflect the essence of India's pluralistic society, where every festival is an opportunity to come together, share joy, and celebrate the richness of life.

Ultimately, Indian festivals act as a unifying force in a diverse and pluralistic society. They celebrate the shared values of love, compassion, and gratitude, and provide a common ground for people of different backgrounds to come together. In a country as vast and varied as India, festivals play a crucial role in maintaining social harmony and promoting a sense of national identity.

As we journey through the myriad festivals of India, we gain a deeper understanding and appreciation of the country's rich cultural heritage. Each festival, with its unique customs and traditions, offers a window into the diverse practices and beliefs that shape the lives of the people. These celebrations are more than just rituals; they are vibrant expressions of the values, histories, and identities of different communities. By participating in or observing these festivals, we see how they contribute to the colourful and intricate tapestry that is India. These celebrations, with their unique customs and traditions, highlight the diverse yet unified nature of Indian society. They teach us that despite our differences, we can find common ground in the shared celebration of life's moments, building lasting bonds and experiencing the beauty of togetherness that unites us all. Through festivals, India exemplifies the idea that diversity is not just a fact of life but a source of strength and resilience, fostering unity in a vibrant, pluralistic society.

CHAPTER III

Art and Craft Traditions

In the heart of India's cultural heritage, where history breathes through ancient temples and the spirit of the land is captured in vibrant hues, there lies a treasure trove of artistic traditions that have flourished for centuries. These traditions passed down from generation to generation, are not just a means of creative expression but a vital thread in the fabric of India's identity.

From the intricate carvings on temple walls that narrate mythological tales to the colourful *rangoli* designs adorning doorsteps during festivals, these artistic traditions are deeply embedded in everyday life. Each region of India boasts its own unique forms of art, whether it be the delicate embroidery of Kashmir, the classical dance forms of *Bharatanatyam* and *Kathak*, or the intricate block printing of Rajasthan. These practices are not merely decorative; they are imbued with cultural significance, often depicting religious stories, historical events, and social customs.

Artistic traditions in India encompass a wide range of disciplines, including painting, sculpture, architecture, dance, music, and literature. Each art form reflects the unique cultural heritage of its region, drawing inspiration from mythology, religion, nature, and daily life. These traditions have evolved over centuries, blending indigenous practices with influences from various invasions, migrations, and cultural exchanges.

For example, Indian classical dance forms like *Bharatanatyam*, *Kathak*, *Odissi*, and *Kuchipudi* trace their origins to ancient temple rituals and storytelling traditions. These dances are characterized by intricate footwork, graceful movements, expressive gestures, and elaborate costumes, all of which contribute to their mesmerizing appeal. Through dance, performers convey stories from Hindu mythology, folklore, and literature, thereby preserving cultural narratives and spiritual teachings.

Similarly, Indian painting traditions, such as *Madhubani*, *Warli*, *Pattachitra*, and *Tanjore*, showcase a rich tapestry of colours, motifs, and symbolism. These paintings often depict scenes from epics like the *Ramayana* and the *Mahabharata*, as well as images of gods, goddesses, and everyday life. Artists use natural materials like vegetable dyes, earth pigments, and gold leaf to create vibrant compositions on various surfaces, including paper, cloth, wood, and walls.

Indian sculpture and architecture also play a significant role in preserving cultural heritage. From the intricate carvings of temples in *Khajuraho* and *Hampi* to the majestic monuments of Delhi's Qutub Minar and Agra's Taj Mahal, Indian architecture reflects a synthesis of indigenous styles with influences from Islamic, Persian, and European traditions. These architectural marvels serve as testaments to India's artistic ingenuity and architectural prowess, attracting visitors from around the world.

Literature is another cornerstone of India's artistic heritage, with a rich tradition of epic poetry, classical literature, folk tales, and modern literature in various languages. The Sanskrit epics like the *Ramayana* and the *Mahabharata*, composed thousands of years ago, continue to inspire writers, poets, and storytellers to this day. These epics are not only revered as sacred texts but also celebrated for their literary excellence, intricate narratives, and profound philosophical insights.

The *Ramayana*, attributed to the sage *Valmiki*, tells the story of Prince *Rama*, his wife *Sita*, and his loyal companion *Hanuman*, exploring themes of duty, righteousness, and devotion. The *Mahabharata*, attributed to *Vyasa*, is a sprawling epic that encompasses the great Kurukshetra War and delves into the moral and ethical dilemmas faced by its characters. These works have been translated into numerous languages and have inspired countless adaptations in literature, theater, and cinema.

Indian literature encompasses a diverse range of themes, reflecting the complexities of human experience. Classical Tamil literature, such as *Sangam* poetry, explores themes of love, war, and social life with remarkable lyrical beauty and emotional depth. Medieval *Bhakti* and Sufi poets like Kabir, Tulsidas, and Amir Khusro infused their works with spiritual fervor and devotion, blending poetic artistry with profound religious insights.

Folk tales and regional literature also play a significant role in India's literary tradition, preserving the oral histories and cultural narratives of various communities. Stories from the *Panchatantra*, *Jataka* tales, and the *Kathasaritsagara* have been passed down through generations, teaching moral lessons and entertaining readers with their wit and wisdom.

In modern times, Indian literature has continued to evolve, addressing contemporary issues and experimenting with new forms and styles. Writers like Rabindranath Tagore, R.K. Narayan, and Arundhati Roy have made significant contributions to global literature, bringing Indian stories and perspectives to an international audience. Their works explore a wide range of themes, from the struggle for independence and social justice to personal identity and existential questions.

Indian literature is a testament to the country's rich cultural and intellectual heritage, offering a window into the diverse experiences and profound insights of its people. Through its vast and varied literary traditions, India continues to celebrate and explore the complexities of life, humanity, and the world.

In essence, India's artistic traditions are a reflection of its cultural diversity, historical richness, and spiritual depth. They serve as bridges between the past and the present, connecting generations and fostering a sense of continuity and belonging. By preserving and celebrating these traditions, India honors its heritage and reaffirms its identity as a cradle of civilization and a beacon of artistic excellence.

Imagine wandering through the narrow lanes of a bustling village, where every corner is a gallery of human creativity. The air is filled with the sound of wooden looms clicking rhythmically, artisans shaping clay with nimble fingers, and painters delicately brushing colours onto canvas. Here, art is not confined to galleries or museums; it lives in the homes, the marketplaces, and the very soul of the people.

In this vibrant village, artistic traditions are not just practiced by a select few; they are woven into the fabric of everyday life. Women sit under the shade of ancient trees, weaving intricate patterns onto vibrant textiles, their hands moving with practiced precision as they create saris, shawls, and scarves that tell stories of tradition and craftsmanship. Nearby, potters mold clay into pots, vases, and figurines, their skilled hands shaping each piece with care and attention to detail.

As you wander further, you come across a group of musicians, their melodies filling the air with rhythm and melody. They play traditional instruments like the *tabla*, *sitar*, and flute, their music echoing through the streets and drawing listeners from far and wide. Around them, dancers twirl and spin, their graceful movements telling tales of love, devotion, and the eternal cycle of life.

In the village marketplace, artisans display their wares with pride, from intricately carved wooden sculptures to brightly painted masks and jewelry adorned with semi-precious stones. Each piece is a testament to the skill and creativity of its maker, reflecting the rich tapestry of cultural influences that shape life in the village.

But perhaps the most striking aspect of this village is the sense of community that pervades every aspect of artistic expression. Families gather to share stories and pass down traditional techniques from one generation to the next. Neighbors come together to celebrate festivals and milestones, with art serving as a common language that transcends differences of language, religion, and caste.

In this village, art is not just a means of livelihood; it is a way of life, a source of joy and inspiration that binds the community together. As you continue your journey through its narrow lanes, you can't help but feel a sense of awe and wonder at the depth of human creativity and the enduring power of artistic expression to uplift the spirit and nourish the soul.

One such art form that catches the eye is Madhubani painting, a tradition rooted in the Mithila region of Bihar. As you step into a humble artist's abode, the walls themselves seem to tell a story. The intricate patterns of flora and fauna, mythological scenes, and everyday village life are depicted in bold, vibrant colours, immediately drawing attention and evoking a sense of wonder.

These paintings are traditionally done by women, who have passed down the techniques and motifs from generation to generation. Each painting is rich with cultural significance and personal expression. The scenes depicted often draw from Hindu mythology, with gods and goddesses like *Krishna*, *Rama*, *Durga*, and *Saraswati* frequently portrayed. These mythological scenes are not just religious depictions but also convey moral stories and cultural values.

The flora and fauna in Madhubani paintings are rendered in a highly stylized manner, showcasing the artist's intimate knowledge of their environment. Common motifs include peacocks, fish, and lotus flowers, each symbolizing various auspicious elements. For instance, fish symbolize fertility and good luck, while the lotus represents purity and divinity.

Beyond their mythological and natural themes, Madhubani paintings also capture the essence of everyday village life. Scenes of people engaged in daily activities, festivals, and rituals provide a vivid portrayal of rural life. These depictions serve as a cultural record, preserving the traditions and lifestyles of the Mithila region for future generations.

The bold, vibrant colours used in Madhubani paintings are derived from natural sources, including turmeric, indigo, and sandalwood. This use of natural dyes not only reflects a deep connection to the environment but also highlights the sustainability practices embedded in traditional art forms. The colours are applied flatly, with no shading, and are often enclosed within intricate patterns, giving the paintings a distinctive and eye-catching appearance.

Each brushstroke in a Madhubani painting is a whisper of history, conveying the collective memory and experiences of the community. These paintings serve as a dialogue with the divine, as many artists create them during religious rituals and festivals, seeking blessings and protection from the deities. The act of painting itself becomes a form of meditation and devotion, connecting the artist with their spiritual beliefs.

Moreover, Madhubani paintings celebrate life's joys and sorrows, capturing the full spectrum of human experience. Weddings, births, harvests, and other significant life events are often depicted with a sense of festivity and reverence, while scenes of mourning or struggle are rendered with equal poignancy. This emotional depth adds to the richness and authenticity of the art form, making each piece a deeply personal and communal expression.

Madhubani painting is more than just an art form; it is a vibrant tradition that encapsulates the cultural, spiritual, and social essence of the Mithila region. Through their intricate patterns and vivid colours, these paintings tell stories that span mythological, natural, and everyday themes, offering a window into the lives and beliefs of the artists. Each artwork is a testament to the enduring legacy and profound beauty of this traditional Indian craft.

In the artist's abode, you witness the meticulous process behind the creation of Madhubani paintings. The artist sits cross-legged on the floor, surrounded by a palette of natural pigments made from crushed stones, minerals, and plant extracts. With a slender brush crafted from bamboo, she dips it into vibrant hues of red, yellow, blue, and green, carefully applying them onto handmade paper or cloth stretched taut on a wooden frame.

As she paints, her movements are deliberate yet fluid, her fingers dancing across the surface with practiced ease. Each stroke is imbued with meaning, drawing inspiration from ancient myths, folklore, and religious motifs. Scenes from the *Ramayana*, *Mahabharata*, and local legends come to life under her skilled hand, evoking a sense of wonder and reverence.

Each Madhubani painting is a piece of love, a testament to the resilience and creativity of its maker. It is a window into a world where art is not separate from life but an integral part of it, where every stroke carries the weight of tradition and the promise of renewal. As you gaze upon the walls adorned with these vibrant masterpieces, you can't help but marvel at the beauty and complexity of the human spirit, expressed so eloquently through the medium of Madhubani painting.

Further south, in the state of Tamil Nadu, the exquisite art of Tanjore painting unfolds its golden brilliance. Imagine walking into a studio where the scent of sandalwood mingles with the faint aroma of paint. Artists, with steady hands and profound concentration, apply gold leaf to richly detailed depictions of Hindu gods and goddesses. These paintings, known for their surface richness and compact composition, are more than just visual spectacles; they are spiritual offerings, capturing the devotion and reverence of their creators. The meticulous process of creating a Tanjore painting, layering gold foil, adding semi-precious stones, and painting with natural dyes, speaks to a tradition deeply intertwined with religious practice and cultural pride.

In the studio, you observe the masterful technique behind Tanjore painting. The artist begins by sketching intricate designs onto a wooden panel or canvas, outlining the figures of deities, celestial beings, and mythological scenes with precision. Next comes the application of gold foil, meticulously cut and adhered to the surface using a special adhesive made from plant resins.

As the gold leaf catches the light, it imparts a radiant glow to the painting, elevating it to a realm of divine splendor. The artist then adds layers of natural dyes, sourced from minerals, vegetables, and flowers, to infuse the composition with vibrant colours and depth. Each brushstroke is deliberate, each hue carefully chosen to evoke a sense of awe and reverence in the viewer.

But Tanjore painting is more than just a visual art form; it is a spiritual practice rooted in devotion and piety. Traditionally, these paintings adorned the walls of temples and palaces, serving as sacred offerings to the gods and goddesses depicted within. They were believed to possess divine energy, capable of bestowing blessings and protection upon the devotees who beheld them.

Today, Tanjore painting continues to be revered as a symbol of cultural heritage and religious devotion in Tamil Nadu and beyond. Artisans pass down the traditional techniques and motifs from one generation to the next, ensuring that this timeless art form remains alive and vibrant in the modern world. Whether displayed in temples, homes, or art galleries, Tanjore paintings serve as reminders of the rich artistic legacy of India and the enduring power of spiritual expression.

In the tribal heartlands of Maharashtra, the simplicity and elegance of Warli art stand in stark contrast to the opulence of Tanjore. Picture a modest village home where walls become canvases for the Warli artists. Using basic geometric shapes, circles, triangles, and squares, they create dynamic scenes of daily life and rituals. The white pigment, derived from rice paste, stands out against the earthy red background, capturing the harmony between humans and nature. Warli art, with its roots in tribal customs, serves not only as decoration but as a medium for preserving social and religious customs. Each Warli painting is a narrative, a visual record of the tribe's collective memory and identity.

In the tranquil setting of a Warli artist's home, you witness the creation of these captivating artworks firsthand. The artist begins by preparing the canvas, a section of the mud-plastered wall, smoothing its surface, and applying a base coat of red ochre or geru, a natural pigment sourced from the earth. With a steady hand and a keen eye for composition, the artist then uses a white pigment made from rice paste or chalk to depict scenes of village life.

The themes of Warli art often revolve around nature, community, and spirituality. Figures of humans, animals, trees, and birds intertwine in rhythmic patterns, conveying a sense of interconnectedness and harmony with the natural world. Rituals like weddings, harvest festivals, and tribal ceremonies are depicted with simplicity and elegance, capturing the essence of tribal life and culture.

What sets Warli art apart is its emphasis on collective identity and communal values. Each painting is a collaborative effort, with multiple artists contributing to its creation, reflecting the communal ethos of the Warli tribe. These artworks are not attributed to individual artists but are seen as expressions of the tribe's shared heritage and worldview.

Warli art serves as a visual language, communicating stories, beliefs, and traditions from one generation to the next. Passed down orally and visually, these narratives provide a link to the tribe's ancestral past, reinforcing a sense of belonging and cultural pride among its members. In this way, Warli paintings serve not only as decorative adornments but as powerful symbols of resilience, resistance, and cultural continuity in the face of modernization and change.

As you gaze upon the walls adorned with Warli art, you are struck by the depth of meaning and simplicity of expression conveyed in each brushstroke. These paintings offer a window into a world where art is not a luxury but a necessity, a means of affirming identity, fostering community, and preserving tradition in the midst of a rapidly changing world.

The rich artistic traditions of India are not limited to paintings. As you traverse the diverse landscapes of the country, you encounter a myriad of crafts that embody the skill and ingenuity of Indian artisans. In the desert state of Rajasthan, the art of embroidery comes alive with intricate patterns and vibrant colours. Picture a group of women sitting together, their hands deftly moving needles through the fabric. Each stitch is a piece of their heritage, a reflection of their community's aesthetic sensibilities. The intricate embroidery, often embellished with mirrors and beads, transforms simple cloth into a tapestry of culture and tradition.

In the bustling villages of Rajasthan, the art of embroidery is a central aspect of daily life. Women gather in communal spaces, often under the shade of ancient trees or in the courtyards of their homes, to engage in this age-old craft. This social gathering is not only a space for creative expression but also a vital part of community life, where stories are shared, skills are passed down, and bonds are strengthened.

With nimble fingers and keen eyes, they work meticulously to create intricate designs inspired by nature, mythology, and the rich cultural heritage of their region. Each design tells a story, whether it's the blooming flowers that symbolize fertility and growth, the majestic peacocks that represent beauty and grace, or the geometric patterns that echo the architectural splendor of Rajasthan's palaces and forts.

Rajasthani embroidery is characterized by its vibrant colours, intricate patterns, and meticulous detailing. The palette is a vivid reflection of the region's natural beauty and festive spirit, featuring bright reds, deep blues, sunny yellows, and lush greens. Each stitch is carefully planned and executed, often following traditional methods that ensure the motifs are both durable and aesthetically pleasing. The use of mirrors, beads, and sequins is a distinctive feature of this embroidery style, adding an extra layer of texture and sparkle to the finished piece. These embellishments catch the light, creating a dazzling effect that enhances the overall beauty of the textiles.

What sets Rajasthani embroidery apart is its deep connection to tradition and community. Many of the motifs and techniques used in this craft have been passed down through generations, with each stitch carrying the wisdom and creativity of those who came before. This heritage is not merely preserved but also celebrated, with each new piece of embroidery serving as a testament to the enduring skills and artistic vision of the community. Embroidery serves not only as a means of artistic expression but also as a way of preserving cultural heritage and fostering social cohesion within the community. It is a living tradition, evolving with each generation yet rooted in timeless practices and communal values.

Beyond its aesthetic appeal, Rajasthani embroidery plays a practical role in everyday life. Embroidered garments, known as *'gota patti'* or *'zari work'*, are worn during special occasions and festivals, adding a touch of elegance and luxury to traditional attire. These garments are often richly adorned, transforming the wearer into a vision of opulence and tradition. Embroidered textiles are also used to adorn home furnishings, including bedspreads, cushion covers, and wall hangings, transforming ordinary spaces into works of art. These items not only beautify homes but also carry the essence of Rajasthani culture into everyday life.

As you witness the artisans at work, you are struck by the dedication and skill that goes into each piece of embroidery. Their hands move with precision and grace, weaving together threads of tradition and innovation to create something truly remarkable. This dedication to their craft ensures that each piece is unique, reflecting both the individual artisan's creativity and the collective heritage of their community. In a world that is increasingly dominated by mass-produced goods, Rajasthani embroidery stands as a testament to the enduring value of craftsmanship, community, and cultural heritage. Each embroidered piece is more than just a decorative item; it is a symbol of identity, a keeper of stories, and a product of a vibrant cultural legacy.

In the serene valleys of Himachal Pradesh, the craft of wood carving tells stories of its own. Imagine the scent of fresh cedar wood in a craftsman's workshop, where delicate chisels carve out elaborate designs on doors, windows, and temple structures. These carvings, often depicting deities, flora, and fauna, are a testament to the region's rich religious and cultural heritage. Each piece of wood, meticulously carved and polished, becomes a tangible link to the past, preserving the artistic legacy of generations.

In the tranquil surroundings of a Himachali woodcarver's workshop, you witness the mastery and precision involved in this age-old craft. The craftsman selects the finest pieces of locally sourced cedar wood, known for its durability and distinctive aroma, and begins the painstaking process of shaping and carving. With skillful hands and keen attention to detail, he brings to life intricate patterns and motifs inspired by the natural beauty and spiritual traditions of the region.

Himachali wood carving is characterized by its intricate designs, flowing curves, and delicate filigree work. Each carving is a labor of love, requiring hours of meticulous craftsmanship and a deep understanding of the medium. From the ornate doorways of ancient temples to the finely crafted furniture found in traditional homes, wood carving is an integral part of Himachali culture, reflecting the region's reverence for nature and its rich artistic heritage.

The themes depicted in Himachali wood carvings are as diverse as the landscapes that inspire them. Carvings of local deities like Lord *Shiva*, Goddess *Durga*, and the snake god *Nag Devta* adorn temple facades and shrine rooms, serving as objects of devotion and spiritual contemplation. Scenes from Hindu folklore and daily life are intricately carved into wooden panels and sculptures, capturing the imagination and storytelling traditions of the region.

But Himachali wood carving is more than just an artistic expression; it is a way of life deeply rooted in the cultural identity of the people. Passed down from father to son and master to apprentice, this ancient craft is a source of pride and livelihood for generations of artisans. It embodies the values of patience, perseverance, and reverence for nature, serving as a reminder of the importance of preserving traditional knowledge and craftsmanship in a rapidly changing world.

As you marvel at the exquisite carvings adorning temples, homes, and public spaces throughout Himachal Pradesh, you can't help but feel a sense of awe at the timeless beauty and spiritual significance of this ancient craft. In a world driven by technology and mass production, Himachali wood carving stands as a testament to the enduring power of human creativity and the timeless allure of handmade craftsmanship.

These diverse art forms, from the delicate embroidery of Rajasthan to the intricate wood carvings of Himachal Pradesh, play a crucial role in preserving and showcasing India's cultural identity. Art in India is not just a pastime; it is a living tradition, a repository of the collective wisdom and creativity of its people. Through their art, Indian artisans keep their heritage alive, passing down stories, beliefs, and practices that define their community.

Art in India serves as a vibrant tapestry woven from threads of tradition, innovation, and cultural exchange. It reflects the country's rich diversity, with each region contributing its unique artistic expressions shaped by its geography, history, and social dynamics. From the intricate patterns of Madhubani paintings to the majestic architecture of ancient temples, Indian art forms serve as windows into the country's past, present, and future.

One of the most remarkable aspects of Indian art is its continuity across generations. Artisans inherit traditional techniques and motifs from their ancestors, honing their skills through years of practice and apprenticeship. This lineage of craftsmanship ensures that ancient art forms like Tanjore painting and Warli art remain vibrant and relevant in the modern world, evolving with the times while retaining their core essence.

Indian art is deeply intertwined with religious and spiritual practices, serving as a medium for devotion, worship, and self-expression. Temples, mosques, and shrines across the country are adorned with intricate carvings, paintings, and sculptures depicting gods, goddesses, and mythological scenes. These sacred artworks not only beautify the sacred spaces but also create an atmosphere of reverence and transcendence, inviting devotees to connect with the divine.

Art in India is also a celebration of community and shared identity. Many art forms, such as Rajasthani embroidery and Himachali wood carving, are deeply rooted in the social fabric of their respective regions. Women gather in groups to embroider garments for weddings and festivals, while artisans collaborate on intricate wood carvings for temples and palaces. These communal practices foster a sense of belonging and solidarity, strengthening bonds within the community.

Furthermore, Indian art serves as a bridge between the past and the present, tradition and modernity. While artisans draw inspiration from ancient motifs and techniques, they also adapt their craft to suit contemporary tastes and lifestyles. This dynamic interplay between tradition and innovation ensures that Indian art remains relevant and dynamic, evolving with the changing times while staying true to its cultural heritage.

In essence, Indian art is a testament to the resilience, creativity, and diversity of the country's people. It reflects their aspirations, values, and aspirations, serving as a mirror to society's evolving hopes and dreams. Through their art, Indian artisans continue to enrich the cultural tapestry of the nation, inspiring awe and admiration in viewers around the world while preserving the timeless beauty of India's artistic heritage.

As you delve deeper into India's artistic traditions, you begin to understand that each piece of art is a window into the soul of the culture that created it. The detailed Madhubani paintings, the golden Tanjore masterpieces, the minimalist Warli designs, and the rich embroidery and carvings all weave together to tell the story of a diverse and vibrant civilization. Through their art, Indians celebrate their past, express their present, and envision their future, ensuring that the legacy of their cultural identity continues to inspire and endure for generations to come.

The beauty of India's artistic heritage lies not only in its aesthetic appeal but also in its profound symbolism and cultural significance. Madhubani paintings, with their intricate motifs and vibrant colours, offer glimpses into ancient myths, folklore, and rituals, preserving the spiritual and cultural traditions of the region. Tanjore paintings, with their opulent gold leaf and rich symbolism, reflect the grandeur and devotion of India's religious and royal traditions, while Warli art, with its simplicity and elegance, embodies the timeless wisdom and community spirit of India's tribal societies.

Furthermore, Indian embroidery and wood carving are not just forms of artistic expression; they are living traditions that connect artisans to their heritage and each other. Through these crafts, communities come together to celebrate festivals, mark milestones, and express their identity, forging bonds of kinship and solidarity that transcend generations. Whether it's the intricate stitches of Rajasthani embroidery or the delicate carvings of Himachali woodwork, each piece of art is imbued with the collective wisdom, creativity, and resilience of its makers.

In conclusion, India's artistic traditions serve as more than just visual representations of creativity, they are living embodiments of the nation's ethos, heritage, and unity. The intricate tapestry of artistic expressions spanning Madhubani paintings, Tanjore masterpieces, Warli designs, and the rich embroidery and wood carvings collectively narrate the story of India's diverse and dynamic civilization.

At the heart of these traditions lies a profound celebration of India's rich cultural tapestry and its ability to adapt and evolve over centuries. From the sacred depictions adorning temple walls to the everyday objects adorned with intricate designs, every piece of art serves as a testament to the depth of India's heritage and the resilience of its people.

Furthermore, India's artistic traditions serve as bridges between generations, connecting the past with the present and paving the way for the future. Through these art forms, Indians not only honor their ancestors and their contributions but also express their own hopes, dreams, and aspirations for the world to see.

Moreover, art in India is a language that transcends the boundaries of time and space, allowing individuals from diverse backgrounds to connect on a deeper level. Whether it's through the shared experience of admiring a centuries-old painting or marveling at the intricacies of a contemporary sculpture, art fosters a sense of unity and understanding among people, regardless of their differences.

As we continue to cherish and preserve these artistic treasures, we ensure that the legacy of India's cultural identity remains a source of inspiration and pride for generations to come. Through nurturing and honoring these traditions, we not only preserve the past but also lay the foundation for a future where creativity, diversity, and unity continue to thrive. In doing so, we uphold the essence of India's artistic heritage as a beacon of cultural richness and timeless creativity for the world to admire and cherish.

CHAPTER IV

A Taste of India's Diversity

As you traverse the diverse landscapes of India, your senses are tantalized by the rich aromas and flavors that fill the air. Each region, with its unique climate, geography, and cultural heritage, offers a culinary journey like no other. From the fiery curries of the south to the aromatic biryanis of the north, every bite tells a story of tradition, innovation, and the unbreakable bond between food and culture.

In the southern states of India, the cuisine is characterized by its bold flavors and generous use of spices. From the tangy tamarind-based dishes of Tamil Nadu to the coconut-infused curries of Kerala, each dish reflects the region's tropical climate and bountiful harvests. Rice, lentils, and coconut form the staple ingredients of many southern dishes, while seafood, fresh vegetables, and aromatic spices add depth and complexity to the flavors.

Traveling northward, you encounter the rich culinary traditions of Punjab, known for its hearty and flavorful dishes. Here, *tandoori* meats, creamy gravies, and butter-laden breads reign supreme, reflecting the region's agrarian heritage and love for hearty meals. Punjabi cuisine is celebrated for its robust flavors and generous use of dairy products like ghee, butter, and yogurt, which lend richness and depth to the dishes.

In the vibrant streets of Rajasthan, the cuisine is a celebration of royal opulence and desert resilience. From the decadent Rajasthani thalis to the fiery *Lal Maas* and the indulgent sweets like *Ghevar* and *Malpua*, every dish is a testament to the region's rich culinary heritage and the resourcefulness of its people. Desert ingredients like millet, lentils, and dried fruits are transformed into hearty meals and delectable sweets, showcasing the ingenuity and creativity of Rajasthani cuisine.

Venturing further east, you discover the diverse culinary landscape of West Bengal, where the flavors of the land and the sea come together in perfect harmony. Bengali cuisine is renowned for its delicate balance of sweet, sour, and spicy flavors, with mustard oil, fresh fish, and aromatic spices playing starring roles in many dishes. From the iconic fish curries to mouthwatering sweets like *Rosgulla* and *Sandesh*, Bengali cuisine is a culinary journey that delights the senses and nourishes the soul.

As you traverse the length and breadth of India, you realize that food is more than just sustenance; it is a reflection of the country's rich cultural tapestry and the diverse influences that have shaped its history. Each region's cuisine tells a story of tradition, innovation, and the enduring bond between food and culture, inviting you to savor the flavors of India's culinary heritage with every delicious bite.

In the southern state of Kerala, the aroma of coconut and spices fills the air as you step into a traditional kitchen. Here, nestled amidst lush greenery and backwaters, the cuisine is a celebration of flavors and textures. Imagine feasting on a traditional Kerala *Sadhya*, a lavish vegetarian meal served on a banana leaf. The centerpiece of the feast is the creamy coconut-based curry, accompanied by an array of side dishes like *avial* (a mixed vegetable curry), *olan* (ash gourd cooked in coconut milk), and *thoran* (stir-fried vegetables with grated coconut). Each dish is a symphony of flavors, blending spicy, sour, sweet, and savory elements in perfect harmony.

As you sit down to enjoy the *Sadhya*, you're struck by the abundance of colours and aromas spread before you. The banana leaf serves as the canvas for this culinary masterpiece, with each dish carefully arranged to create a visual feast for the eyes as well as the palate. You start by mixing the various curries and side dishes with the fluffy mound of rice in the center of the leaf, savoring the complex interplay of flavors with each bite.

The creamy *avial*, with its medley of vegetables cooked to perfection in a coconut-yogurt gravy, provides a cooling contrast to the fiery tang of the spicy *rasam*, a traditional Kerala soup made with tamarind, tomatoes, and aromatic spices. The subtly sweet *olan*, delicately flavored with pumpkin and coconut milk, adds a touch of richness to the meal, while the crunchy thoran, bursting with the freshness of green beans, cabbage, or carrots, provides a satisfying crunch.

But the star of the *Sadhya* is undoubtedly the velvety coconut curry, known as "*Ishtu*" or "Kerala Stew." Made with creamy coconut milk, fragrant spices, and tender vegetables like potatoes, carrots, and peas, this dish epitomizes the essence of Kerala cuisine simple yet indulgent, comforting yet flavorful. With each spoonful of stew, you're transported to the tranquil backwaters of Kerala, where the rhythm of life is as gentle and soothing as the flavors of the food.

As you savor the last morsels of the *Sadhya*, you're filled with a sense of contentment and gratitude for the culinary traditions of Kerala. The *Sadhya* is not just a meal; it's a cultural experience, a celebration of community, and a testament to the rich culinary heritage of the region. As you bid farewell to the traditional kitchen, you carry with you the memories of flavors and aromas that will linger in your senses long after the meal is over.

Further elaborating on the experience, you find that the *Sadhya* is not just about the food itself, but also about the rituals and traditions that accompany it. The act of serving and eating the *Sadhya* is steeped in symbolism and etiquette, reflecting the values of hospitality, generosity, and community that are deeply ingrained in Kerala culture. Each dish is served in a specific order, with guests encouraged to eat with their hands to fully experience the textures and flavors of the food. As you partake in these rituals, you feel a sense of connection to the centuries-old customs that have been passed down through generations, uniting people in a shared appreciation for good food and company.

As you delve even further into the captivating world of Delhi's street food culture, you uncover layers of history, tradition, and innovation that enrich the experience of indulging in chaat.

Chandni Chowk, with its labyrinthine lanes and centuries-old architecture, becomes more than just a setting for your culinary adventure it's a living museum of Delhi's past, where each corner holds secrets waiting to be discovered. As you navigate through the chaotic yet mesmerizing maze of the market, you find yourself immersed in a sensory symphony unlike any other. The vibrant colours of the stalls, the rhythmic clang of utensils, and the tantalizing aromas wafting through the air create an intoxicating atmosphere that heightens your anticipation.

At the chaat stall, you witness the skilled craftsmanship of the vendors as they expertly assemble each *golgappa* with precision and finesse. Their hands move with a fluidity born of years of practice, turning simple ingredients into culinary masterpieces. It's not just about the food it's about the passion and dedication that go into every dish, the pride of showcasing Delhi's gastronomic heritage to eager patrons.

As you take your first bite of the *golgappa*, you're transported on a journey of flavors that spans centuries of culinary evolution. The crispness of the puri gives way to the burst of tangy potato and chickpea filling, perfectly complemented by the sweetness of the tamarind chutney and the heat of the green chili. It's a symphony of tastes and textures that dances on your palate, leaving you craving more with each mouthful.

But perhaps the most remarkable aspect of the chaat experience is its ability to transcend boundaries and bring people together. As you stand in line with fellow food enthusiasts from all walks of life, you're struck by the sense of unity and camaraderie that permeates the air. Here, amidst the chaos of the market, strangers become friends as they bond over their shared love of good food and great company.

And as you bid farewell to Chandni Chowk and the unforgettable flavors of Delhi's street food, you carry with you not just the memories of a delicious meal, but a deeper appreciation for the rich tapestry of culture and history that defines the city. For in the bustling streets and bustling markets of Delhi, food isn't just sustenance it's a celebration of life, a testament to resilience, and a reminder that the true essence of a city lies in its people and their stories.

Beyond the surface of traditional Gujarati cuisine lies a world of culinary wonders waiting to be explored. From the bustling markets of Ahmedabad to the quaint villages dotting the countryside, every corner of Gujarat offers a unique gastronomic experience.

Picture yourself wandering through the vibrant streets of Ahmedabad's old city, where food vendors line the narrow lanes, offering a dizzying array of snacks and sweets. Here, you can indulge in the crispy goodness of *fafda* and *jalebi*, a classic combination that perfectly balances sweet and savory flavors. Or perhaps you're drawn to the spicy aromas wafting from a nearby chaat stall, where you can sample a variety of tangy and tantalizing street snacks like *sev puri, dabeli,* and *papdi chaat.*

As you venture further into the heartland of Gujarat, you find yourself surrounded by the lush greenery of the countryside, where traditional farming practices have long been the backbone of the local economy. Here, you can experience the true essence of Gujarati cuisine, with its emphasis on fresh, seasonal ingredients and simple yet flavorful cooking techniques.

Imagine sitting down to a home-cooked meal in a rustic farmhouse, surrounded by fields of wheat, mustard, and sugarcane. Here, you're treated to a feast of regional delicacies, from the hearty warmth of *undhiyu* a traditional mixed vegetable stew to the delicate sweetness of *shrikhand*, a creamy dessert made from strained yogurt and flavored with saffron and cardamom.

And let's not forget about the rich cultural tapestry that informs every aspect of Gujarati cuisine. From the colourful festivals that mark the changing seasons to the age-old traditions of hospitality and generosity, Gujarat's culinary heritage is deeply intertwined with its social and cultural fabric.

As you savor each mouthful of Gujarati delicacies, you can't help but feel a sense of connection to the land, to the people, and to the timeless traditions that have shaped Gujarat's culinary identity. And as you bid farewell to this culinary paradise, you carry with you not just the memories of unforgettable meals, but a newfound appreciation for the richness and diversity of Indian cuisine.

As you journey eastwards to the culturally rich state of West Bengal, the cuisine opens up a new world of flavors and aromas. Here, in the land of rivers and deltas, seafood holds a special place in the hearts and palates of the locals. The lush landscape, crisscrossed by rivers, provides an abundance of fresh fish and other aquatic delights that form the cornerstone of Bengali cuisine.

Picture yourself seated by the banks of the Hooghly River, indulging in a plate of piping hot fish curry served with fragrant rice. The curry, prepared with fresh catch from the river, mustard oil, and a blend of aromatic spices, is not just a dish but a reflection of the region's deep-rooted maritime heritage. Mustard oil imparts a distinctive sharpness, while spices like turmeric, cumin, and coriander create a complex and inviting aroma. Each spoonful is a symphony of flavors, offering a glimpse into centuries of trade and tradition that have shaped West Bengal's culinary legacy. The local fish, such as *rohu* or *hilsa*, is often marinated with turmeric and salt before being cooked, ensuring that every bite is succulent and flavorful.

Continuing your culinary exploration, you venture into the bustling streets of Kolkata, where the vibrant street food scene captivates your senses. Amidst the hustle and bustle, you discover Kolkata's beloved street food specialty, *puchka*. Similar to the *Golgappas* of the North. These crispy, hollow spheres filled with a spicy and tangy concoction of tamarind water, potatoes, and chickpeas are a true delight for the taste buds. As you sample one after another, you're enchanted by the explosion of flavors that epitomize

Kolkata's street food culture. The tanginess of the tamarind, the heat of the spices, and the crunch of the puchka shell combine to create an unforgettable sensory experience. Street vendors, known for their skill and speed, prepare *puchkas* fresh on the spot, ensuring that each one is perfectly crisp and bursting with flavor.

But West Bengal's gastronomic delights extend beyond seafood and street food. The state is renowned for its rich tradition of sweets and desserts, with iconic treats like *rasgulla*, *Sandesh*, and *mishti doi* stealing the spotlight. Crafted from fresh cottage cheese, and sugar, and infused with aromatic spices like cardamom and saffron, these sweets are more than just desserts; they are a celebration of life's sweetness and joys. Rasgulla, soft and spongy balls soaked in a light sugar syrup, offer a delicate sweetness and a melt-in-your-mouth texture. Sandesh, often flavored with mango or rose water, showcases the versatility of *chhena* (cottage cheese) in creating subtly sweet and creamy confections. *Mishti doi*, a fermented sweet yogurt, provides a refreshing and tangy counterpoint to the other desserts, its creamy texture and caramelized sweetness making it a beloved end to any meal.

As you bid farewell to the land of rivers and deltas, you carry with you not just the memories of delectable meals, but a profound appreciation for the culinary diversity and richness of India's cultural mosaic. Each taste, aroma, and texture encountered during your culinary journey becomes a part of your being, weaving itself into the fabric of your memories and shaping your understanding of the world. The culinary traditions of West Bengal, with their unique blend of historical influences and local ingredients, offer a window into the soul of the region. They remind you that food is not just sustenance but a connection to culture, history, and community and that every meal is a story waiting to be told.

With each dish savored and recipe shared, you come to understand that food is more than just sustenance; it is a language of its own, capable of conveying emotions, histories, and identities. The flavors of Kerala's coconut-infused curries, Delhi's spicy *chaats*, Gujarat's wholesome *dhoklas*, West Bengal's seafood delights, and Punjab's indulgent gravies linger on your palate, serving as reminders of the diverse tapestry of flavors that make up India's culinary landscape.

And as you continue your journey, you do so with a newfound reverence for the power of food to nourish not only the body but also the soul. In every shared meal and communal feast, you witness the transformative power of food to bridge cultures and bring people together in shared culinary experiences. Whether it's sitting down with strangers in a bustling street food market or being welcomed into the warmth of a family kitchen, you come to realize that food has the remarkable ability to transcend boundaries and forge connections that transcend language, religion, and nationality.

With each new dish tasted and recipe learned, you become a custodian of India's culinary heritage, carrying forward the traditions and flavors of this rich and diverse land. And as you journey onwards, you do so with a deep sense of gratitude for the myriad ways in which food has enriched your life, opening your eyes and your palate to the infinite possibilities of the culinary world. In the end, it is not just the food that sustains us, but the stories, memories, and connections that we share around the table that truly nourish the soul.

Imagine stepping into a bustling Punjabi *dhaba*, where the air is thick with the tantalizing aroma of spices and freshly baked bread. The vibrant colours of the decor and the lively chatter of patrons create an atmosphere of warmth and camaraderie. Here, in the heart of Punjab, food is not merely sustenance; it is a symbol of abundance, hospitality, and community.

As you settle into your seat, the friendly waiter brings forth a piping hot basket of tandoori rotis, their golden brown crusts glistening with ghee. The aroma of charred edges and smoky flavors fills the air, teasing your senses and whetting your appetite. Alongside the *rotis* comes a selection of rich and creamy gravies, each one a masterpiece of flavor and texture.

But it is the iconic butter chicken that steals the spotlight, its vibrant orange hue and velvety consistency beckoning you to indulge. As you take your first bite, your taste buds are greeted by a symphony of flavors, the tanginess of tomatoes, the richness of cream, and the subtle heat of spices. The tender pieces of chicken, marinated in a blend of yogurt and spices, practically melt in your mouth, leaving behind a lingering sensation of comfort and satisfaction.

Accompanying the butter chicken are fluffy naan bread and fragrant basmati rice, their subtle flavors providing the perfect foil to the boldness of the curry. The soft, pillowy texture of the naan, with its slightly charred edges, serves as the ideal vessel for scooping up the creamy sauce. The delicate aroma of the basmati rice, infused with the essence of saffron and cardamom, adds a touch of elegance to the meal.

As you savor each mouthful, you can't help but marvel at the culinary mastery that goes into creating such a dish.

From the careful selection of spices to the meticulous balance of flavors, every element of the butter chicken speaks to the rich culinary heritage of Punjab. It is a dish that embodies the spirit of the land, bold, vibrant, and full of life.

But more than just a meal, butter chicken is a celebration of Punjab's vibrant and flavorful cuisine. It is a testament to the region's rich agricultural bounty and its tradition of hospitality and generosity. As you sit back, content and satisfied, you can't help but feel grateful for the opportunity to experience firsthand the culinary delights of this vibrant northern state.

As you delve deeper into the diverse cuisines of India, you begin to unravel the intricate layers of culture, tradition, and community that are woven into every dish. Each culinary creation tells a story that transcends mere ingredients and cooking techniques; it is a narrative of the land it originates from, the people who have lovingly prepared it for generations, and the shared experiences that have shaped its evolution.

In the southern regions of India, where the sun-drenched coasts meet lush tropical forests, the cuisine reflects the bounty of the land and the rich cultural heritage of its people. Fiery curries bursting with spices, tangy chutneys made from fresh tropical fruits, and aromatic rice dishes cooked in coconut milk are just a few examples of the vibrant flavors that characterize southern Indian cuisine. Here, food is not just a means of sustenance; it is a celebration of life, a reflection of the region's agricultural abundance, and a testament to the ingenuity of its people.

Traveling northwards, you encounter the bustling streets of Delhi and the savory delights of its famous chaats. From the crisp papdi topped with spicy potatoes and tangy chutneys to the succulent *tikkis* garnished with yogurt and mint, each bite is a burst of flavor that reflects the vibrant street food culture of the capital city. In Delhi, food is a social affair, a means of bringing people together in shared culinary experiences and forging bonds of friendship and camaraderie.

Further west, in the arid deserts of Rajasthan the cuisine is a testament to the resourcefulness of its people and their ability to create delicious meals with limited ingredients. Dishes like *dal baati churma*, a hearty combination of lentils, baked wheat balls, and sweetened crumbs, speak to the region's harsh environment and the resilience of its inhabitants. In Rajasthan, food is not just about sustenance; it is a symbol of resilience, community, and the indomitable spirit of its people.

And in the lush green valleys of Kashmir, where snow-capped mountains meet pristine lakes, the cuisine reflects the region's natural beauty and the rich cultural tapestry of its inhabitants. Fragrant rice dishes cooked with saffron and spices, tender meat curries flavored with aromatic herbs, and delicate desserts made from fresh fruits and nuts are just a few examples of the culinary delights that await you in Kashmir. Here, food is a celebration of nature, a tribute to the bounty of the land, and a reflection of the region's deep-rooted traditions and customs.

As you embark on your culinary journey through the diverse landscapes of India, you're immediately struck by the realization that food is not merely sustenance; it's a gateway to understanding the intricate tapestry of cultures, traditions, and communities that define this vibrant nation. Every dish served on the table is a story waiting to be told, a narrative woven with threads of history, geography, and human connection.

In the bustling streets of Mumbai, as you bite into a spicy vada pav or savor the tangy flavors of *pav bhaji,* you're transported into the heart of Maharashtra's bustling metropolis. These iconic street foods are more than just snacks; they're a reflection of Mumbai's vibrant culture, its fast-paced lifestyle, and its spirit of resilience in the face of adversity. Each bite is a tribute to the ingenuity and resourcefulness of the city's inhabitants, who have transformed humble ingredients into culinary masterpieces that delight the senses and nourish the soul.

As you travel southwards to the coastal regions of Kerala, you're greeted by the aroma of coconut and spices wafting through the air. Here, amidst the swaying palm trees and backwaters, food is a celebration of nature's bounty and the rich cultural heritage of the region. From the fragrant seafood curries to the fluffy *appams* served with creamy coconut milk, each dish tells a story of Kerala's deep-rooted connection to its land and its people. It's a testament to the resilience of Kerala's inhabitants, who have thrived in harmony with their environment for centuries, creating dishes that are as nourishing for the body as they are for the soul.

In the colourful markets of Rajasthan, where vibrant textiles and intricate handicrafts line the streets, food is a feast for the senses. Here, amidst the desert sands and ancient forts, the cuisine reflects the region's arid climate and the resourcefulness of its people. From the hearty *dal baati churma* to the spicy *laal maas*, each dish is a testament to Rajasthan's rich culinary heritage and its tradition of hospitality. It's a celebration of Rajasthan's vibrant culture, its rich history, and its indomitable spirit in the face of adversity.

As you journey through the lush green valleys of Himachal Pradesh, where snow-capped mountains and pristine rivers abound, you discover a world of flavors waiting to be explored. Here, amidst the tranquil beauty of the Himalayas, food is a celebration of life's simple pleasures and the bond between family and community. From the hearty *thukpa* to the fragrant *siddu*, each dish is a reflection of Himachal's rich cultural heritage and its deep connection to the land. It's a tribute to the resilience of Himachal's inhabitants, who have carved out a life amidst the rugged terrain and harsh climate, creating dishes that are as hearty as they are delicious.

India's culinary heritage is not just a collection of recipes but a living tradition that evolves with time, influenced by trade, invasions, and cultural exchanges. It's a celebration of unity in diversity, where each dish tells a story of the land and its people. Through food, we see the ingenuity of Indian homemakers, the creativity of chefs, and the resilience of communities adapting to their environment and preserving their heritage. In every bite, there's a piece of history, a burst of culture, and a testament to the spirit of unity that binds this incredible nation. The diversity of Indian cuisine is a mirror to its society, reflecting a mosaic of flavors that come together to form a harmonious whole.

CHAPTER V

Traditional Clothing and Textiles

In the vibrant mosaic of India's cultural tapestry, traditional clothing, and textiles stand as eloquent testimonies to the nation's rich heritage and storied past. Embarking on a journey into the realm of Indian attire reveals a kaleidoscope of garments, each intricately woven with threads of tradition, craftsmanship, and identity.

At the heart of Indian attire lies a deep reverence for tradition and heritage, with garments often serving as symbolic representations of regional customs and beliefs. From the colourful *sarees* of the south to the majestic turbans of the north, each attire carries with it the legacy of generations, preserving age-old techniques and designs passed down through the ages.

Take, for example, the iconic saree, a symbol of grace and elegance that transcends regional boundaries. Woven from luxurious silk or lightweight cotton, and adorned with intricate patterns and embellishments, the saree embodies the essence of Indian femininity and tradition. Each fold of the fabric whispers tales of craftsmanship and artistry, reflecting the diverse cultural influences that have shaped its evolution over the centuries.

Similarly, the vibrant hues and elaborate embroidery of the Punjabi suit evoke a sense of joy and celebration, mirroring the exuberant spirit of Punjab's folk culture. From the intricately embroidered phulkari dupattas to the colourful patterns of the *salwar kameez*, every element of the Punjabi suit reflects the region's vivacious personality for life.

Beyond their aesthetic appeal, Indian garments also serve as potent symbols of identity and belonging. The crisp white dhoti worn by men in southern India embodies simplicity and humility, while the ornate *lehenga choli* of Rajasthan reflects the region's royal legacy and opulent heritage.

In every stitch and seam, Indian attire encapsulates the essence of a nation, weaving together threads of tradition, craftsmanship, and cultural pride. As you immerse yourself in the world of Indian clothing and textiles, you find yourself enchanted by the beauty and diversity of this ancient art form, each garment a testament to India's enduring legacy of creativity and craftsmanship.

Immerse yourself in the bustling markets of Varanasi, where the ancient art of silk weaving has thrived for centuries. Here, amidst the rhythmic clacking of looms and the vibrant hues of silk threads, you uncover the timeless elegance of the Banarasi saree. Adorned with intricate patterns of *zari* and *meenakari* work, these sarees transcend mere garments; they embody a legacy of luxury, grace, and tradition.

The *Banarasi saree* is a treasure trove of cultural heritage, intricately woven into the fabric of Uttar Pradesh's history. Its origins can be traced back to the Mughal era when skilled artisans were commissioned to create opulent fabrics for royalty. Over the centuries, the art of *Banarasi* weaving has been honed and perfected, passed down through generations of master craftsmen who imbue each saree with their expertise and dedication.

Wearing a *Banarasi saree* is not just a fashion statement; it is a celebration of tradition and craftsmanship. Brides adorn these exquisite sarees on their wedding day, symbolizing purity, grace, and prosperity. Each saree is a work of art, meticulously crafted with intricate motifs inspired by nature, mythology, and Mughal architecture. The shimmering *zari* threads add a touch of opulence, while the delicate *meenakari* work infuses the fabric with vibrant colours and intricate designs.

But the allure of the *Banarasi saree* extends far beyond bridal attire. It is a symbol of status and sophistication, cherished by women of all ages and backgrounds. Whether worn for festive occasions, cultural ceremonies, or everyday elegance, the *Banarasi* saree exudes timeless beauty and understated glamour.

As you navigate the labyrinthine streets of Varanasi, surrounded by the sights and sounds of centuries-old craftsmanship, you can't help but marvel at the enduring legacy of the *Banarasi saree*. It is more than just a piece of fabric; it is a living testament to the artistic prowess and cultural richness of Uttar Pradesh, woven into the very fabric of its identity.

In the bustling markets of Kanchipuram, the renowned silk sarees of Tamil Nadu await your discovery. The Kanchipuram *saree*, also known as the *Kanchi saree*, stands as a pinnacle of the region's rich textile tradition, celebrated for its opulent textures and intricate designs. Each saree is a masterpiece of craftsmanship, meticulously woven with motifs inspired by temple architecture, mythology, and religious symbolism.

The weaving of Kanchipuram sarees is steeped in tradition, with techniques passed down through generations of skilled artisans. It's not just a craft; it's a way of life, with weavers dedicating themselves to the meticulous process of handloom weaving. The *sarees* are typically woven with pure mulberry silk threads, known for their strength and luster, giving the fabric its characteristic sheen and drape.

One of the defining features of Kanchipuram sarees is their elaborate borders, intricately embellished with motifs such as temple sculptures, peacocks, floral patterns, and mythical creatures like the *yali* (a mythical lion). These motifs hold deep cultural significance, reflecting the region's rich heritage and spiritual beliefs. For example, the peacock motif symbolizes fertility and prosperity, while the *yali* represents strength and protection.

Beyond their aesthetic appeal, *Kanchipuram sarees* hold profound cultural and religious significance. They are often worn by brides on their wedding day, symbolizing purity, grace, and auspiciousness. Each *saree* is believed to carry the blessings of the gods, making it a cherished heirloom passed down through generations.

The journey to procure a Kanchipuram saree is an experience in itself, with buyers immersing themselves in the vibrant atmosphere of the silk markets, where weavers showcase their latest creations. Here, amidst the hustle and bustle, you witness firsthand the dedication and skill that goes into crafting each *saree*, from the intricate design process to the painstaking weaving technique.

As you drape yourself in the luxurious folds of a *Kanchipuram saree*, you feel a profound sense of connection to the rich cultural tapestry of Tamil Nadu. It's not just a garment; it's a symbol of heritage, tradition, and timeless elegance. And as you admire its intricate beauty, you can't help but marvel at the enduring legacy of the *Kanchipuram saree,* a true masterpiece of Indian craftsmanship.

As you venture into the serene valleys of Kashmir, a land renowned for its breathtaking natural beauty, you are enveloped by an atmosphere of tranquility and awe-inspiring vistas. Here, amidst the snow-capped peaks and verdant meadows, you discover the exquisite allure of *Pashmina* shawls, crafted with utmost care and skill by Kashmiri weavers.

At the heart of these luxurious shawls lies the fine wool of the *Changthangi* goat, a breed native to the high-altitude regions of Ladakh. Renowned for its exceptional softness and warmth, *Pashmina* wool is painstakingly harvested and meticulously woven into the fabric of Kashmir's cultural heritage. Each shawl is a testament to the enduring bond between the people of Kashmir and their natural surroundings, embodying a legacy of craftsmanship that has been passed down through generations.

The process of crafting a *Pashmina* shawl is a labor of love, requiring meticulous attention to detail and unwavering dedication. From the spinning of the yarn to the intricate weaving of delicate patterns, every step is executed with precision and care. It is this commitment to quality and craftsmanship that sets Pashmina shawls apart, making them highly sought after by connoisseurs of luxury and elegance worldwide.

Adorned with intricate designs inspired by Kashmir's rich cultural heritage, *Pashmina* shawls are more than just garments; they are works of art that tell a story of tradition, beauty, and craftsmanship. From the graceful paisleys to the delicate motifs of flowers and chinar leaves, each design is imbued with symbolism and meaning, reflecting the region's deep-rooted cultural heritage and artistic sensibility.

As you wrap yourself in the soft folds of a *Pashmina* shawl, you are not just enveloped in warmth and comfort; you are also enveloped in the rich tapestry of Kashmir's history and culture. It is a feeling of connection to a land steeped in tradition and beauty, where every thread tells a story of resilience, creativity, and the timeless allure of nature's bounty.

As you navigate through the rugged terrain of Rajasthan, a land of stark contrasts and vibrant colours, you are immediately drawn to the mesmerizing beauty of *Bandhani* textiles. Originating from the arid desert regions of western India, *Bandhani* fabrics captivate the senses with their bold hues and intricate tie-dye patterns, offering a glimpse into the rich cultural tapestry of the region.

> *"Bandhani, derived from the Sanskrit word bandhan, meaning "to tie," is an age-old textile art form that has been practiced for centuries by skilled artisans in Rajasthan. The process of creating Bandhani textiles involves a meticulous technique known as "resist dyeing," where small portions of fabric are tied tightly with thread before being submerged into vibrant dyes. As the fabric is dyed and the threads are removed, intricate patterns emerge, ranging from geometric shapes to floral motifs, reminiscent of the mesmerizing patterns found in nature."*

What sets *Bandhani* textiles apart is not just their exquisite craftsmanship, but also the symbolism and cultural significance embedded within each piece. Traditionally, *Bandhani* fabrics were worn on auspicious occasions such as weddings, festivals, and religious ceremonies, symbolizing prosperity, happiness, and good fortune. The vibrant colours and intricate patterns of *Bandhani* textiles serve as a visual representation of Rajasthan's rich cultural heritage and the resilience of its people, who have adapted their traditional craft to thrive in a harsh and unforgiving environment.

Beyond their aesthetic appeal, *Bandhani* textiles also hold economic importance for the communities that produce them. Artisans, often women, play a central role in the creation of *Bandhani* fabrics, passing down their skills and techniques from generation to generation. Through their craftsmanship, they not only preserve an ancient tradition but also sustain livelihoods and foster community resilience in the face of economic challenges.

As you immerse yourself in the world of *Bandhani* textiles, you can't help but marvel at the intricate artistry and cultural depth embodied in each fabric. From the vibrant colours that evoke the spirit of Rajasthan's landscapes to the intricate tie-dye patterns that tell stories of tradition and craftsmanship, *Bandhani* textiles are more than just garments; they are a living testament to the enduring legacy of Rajasthan's cultural heritage.

As you venture into the verdant hills of Assam, you are enchanted by the allure of *Muga* silk, a fabric renowned for its unparalleled beauty and remarkable durability. Nestled amidst the lush greenery of this picturesque region, *Muga* silk stands as a testament to the rich textile heritage of Assam and the skilled craftsmanship of its artisans.

Muga silk, derived from the silk produced by the Antheraea assamensis silkworm, is prized for its natural golden hue, which sets it apart from other varieties of silk. This distinctive colour is achieved without any artificial dyes, making *Muga* silk truly unique and highly coveted in the world of textiles. The process of harvesting and weaving *Muga* silk is labor-intensive and time-consuming, requiring meticulous care and precision at every stage.

Skilled artisans, often from rural communities in Assam, are responsible for the intricate process of transforming

Muga silk into exquisite sarees and *mekhela chadors*, traditional Assamese garments worn by women. These artisans possess a deep understanding of the silk-making process, which has been passed down through generations within their families. From rearing the silkworms to spinning the silk yarn and weaving the fabric, each step is carried out with precision and reverence for the centuries-old tradition.

What sets Muga silk apart is not just its natural beauty, but also its exceptional durability and longevity. Known as one of the strongest natural fibers, *Muga silk sarees* and *mekhela chadors* are cherished heirlooms that can be passed down through generations. The fabric retains its luster and resilience over time, making it a symbol of prestige and sophistication in Assamese culture.

Beyond its aesthetic and practical qualities, *Muga* silk holds deep cultural significance for the people of Assam. It is often worn on special occasions such as weddings, festivals, and religious ceremonies, symbolizing purity, prosperity, and tradition. The intricate motifs and designs woven into *Muga* silk garments reflect the rich cultural heritage of Assam, with patterns inspired by nature, mythology, and local customs.

As you admire the timeless beauty of *Muga* silk amidst the lush green hills of Assam, you are reminded of the enduring legacy of craftsmanship and tradition that defines this region. Each piece of *Muga* silk is not just a garment; it is a work of art, a testament to the skill, dedication, and cultural richness of Assam's textile traditions.

Traditional Indian clothing embodies the rich tapestry of the nation's cultural heritage. From the opulent *Banarasi sarees* to the intricate *Kanchipuram sarees* and the vibrant *Bandhani* textiles, each garment tells a story of tradition, craftsmanship, and identity. Woven into the fabric of India's history, these clothes serve as symbols of pride and connection, bridging the past with the present and inspiring future generations to cherish and preserve their cultural legacy.

CHAPTER VI

Music and Dance: Rhythms of India

In the vivid mosaic of India's cultural tapestry, music and dance emerge as vibrant threads, weaving together the essence of the nation's profound traditions, historical depth, and spiritual richness. They stand not merely as art forms but as profound expressions of India's collective soul, carrying within them the echoes of centuries-old stories, emotions, and spiritual yearnings.

Immerse yourself in the rhythmic beats and graceful gestures of Indian classical arts, and we'll find ourselves drawn into a realm where time seems to stand still. Here, amidst the intricate footwork and emotive expressions, lies a universe of beauty and storytelling that resonates across generations and transcends geographical boundaries.

Begin our exploration in the sanctified environs of southern India, where the ancient temples of Tamil Nadu echo with the strains of Carnatic music and the mesmerizing movements of *Bharatanatyam* dancers. Steeped in mythology and spiritual devotion, *Bharatanatyam* is more than a dance; it's a sacred journey that transports both performers and audiences alike to realms of divine ecstasy and human emotion. Through its graceful movements, expressive gestures, and evocative facial expressions, *Bharatanatyam* becomes a conduit for storytelling, weaving together tales of gods, goddesses, and mythical heroes with a symphony of movement and rhythm.

Travel northward to the historic city of Lucknow, where the grandeur of Mughal courts finds expression in the graceful spins and intricate footwork of *Kathak* dancers. Originating from the ancient tradition of storytelling through dance, *Kathak* is a fusion of poetry, music, and movement that celebrates the beauty of life and the human experience. With its dynamic compositions and subtle nuances, *Kathak* becomes a canvas for exploring themes of love, longing, and spiritual devotion, captivating audiences with its elegance and depth.

Continue our journey to the eastern state of Odisha, where the tranquil ambiance of temple precincts is enlivened by the lyrical movements of *Odissi* dancers. Rooted in the devotional rituals of temple worship, *Odissi* is a dance form that embodies grace, fluidity, and spiritual fervor. Through its intricate choreography and emotive expressions, *Odissi* becomes a medium for storytelling, narrating tales of love, mythology, and divine communion with a captivating blend of movement and emotion.

As we delve deeper into the rich tapestry of India's classical arts, we'll find ourselves mesmerized by the intricate *ragas* of Hindustani music, the soul-stirring beats of folk rhythms, and the effervescent energy of Bollywood dance. Each genre, with its distinct style and flavor, contributes to the kaleidoscope of India's cultural heritage, enriching it with layers of melody, rhythm, and emotion.

In the vibrant tapestry of India's cultural heritage, music and dance are not mere performances; they are profound expressions of the country's soul, carrying within them the echoes of its past, the emotions of its present, and the aspirations of its future. Through their rhythmic cadences and graceful movements, Indian classical arts become a timeless bridge that connects hearts, minds, and spirits, transcending the boundaries of time and space to weave a narrative of beauty, emotion, and storytelling that resonates across generations.

As we step into the traditional dance studio nestled amidst the bustling streets of Chennai, we are immediately enveloped in a world of enchantment and beauty. The air is filled with the mellifluous strains of classical Carnatic music, resonating with the timeless rhythms of ancient Tamil Nadu. Each note reverberates through the space, creating an ethereal ambiance that transports us to a realm where time seems to stand still.

Amidst this musical symphony, our gaze falls upon a group of dancers adorned in resplendent costumes, their movements fluid and graceful like the gentle sway of palm trees in the breeze. They are practitioners of *Bharatanatyam*, the quintessential classical dance form that traces its origins to the sacred temples of southern India. But *Bharatanatyam* is more than just a dance; it is a sacred art, a spiritual journey that transcends the realms of the physical and the divine.

As we watch with rapt attention, the dancers begin to weave their magic, their bodies becoming vessels for storytelling, their gestures imbued with profound meaning and emotion. With each intricate footwork and expressive hand gesture, they bring to life the ancient tales of gods, goddesses, and mythical heroes that have been passed down through generations. Through the language of movement and expression, they evoke a sense of reverence and awe, transporting audiences to realms of divine ecstasy and human emotion.

The essence of *Bharatanatyam* lies not only in its technical prowess but also in its ability to evoke deep emotions and spiritual resonance. Every movement is imbued with symbolism, every gesture pregnant with meaning, as the dancers delve into the rich tapestry of

Indian mythology and folklore. From the graceful movements of the *Ardhamandala* to the fierce expressions of the *Nataraja* pose, each element of *Bharatanatyam* tells a story, weaving together threads of tradition, culture, and spirituality into a mesmerizing visual tapestry.

As the performance unfolds before our eyes, we find ourselves drawn into a world of beauty, grace, and transcendence. The boundaries between the mundane and the divine blur as we are swept away by the sheer artistry and spiritual depth of *Bharatanatyam*. In this sacred space, where music and movement converge, we experience a profound sense of connection to something greater than ourselves – to the timeless heritage of southern India, to the universal language of art, and to the eternal dance of creation itself.

And as the final notes of the music fade into silence, we are left with a lingering sense of awe and wonder, as if touched by the divine. In the hallowed halls of the traditional dance studio in Chennai, we have witnessed not just a performance, but a spiritual journey – a testament to the enduring power of *Bharatanatyam* to inspire, uplift, and transform both the dancer and the audience alike.

As we embark on our journey northwards to the historic city of Lucknow, known for its rich cultural heritage and architectural splendor, we find ourselves captivated by the mesmerizing rhythms and intricate footwork of *Kathak*, a classical dance form deeply rooted in the traditions of northern India.

Originating in the opulent courts of medieval India, *Kathak* has its roots in the temple traditions of northern India, where it evolved as a vibrant expression of devotion and spiritual fervor. Over the centuries, *Kathak* underwent a fascinating evolution, assimilating influences from various cultures and traditions, including Persian, Mughal, and Hindu, to emerge as a sophisticated art form that celebrates the beauty of life, love, and the human experience.

As we enter a traditional *Kathak* dance studio in Lucknow, we're immediately struck by the elegance and grace of the dancers, who effortlessly navigate the space with precision and poise. Each movement, whether a delicate gesture or a swift spin, is executed with meticulous attention to detail, reflecting years of rigorous training and dedication.

The rhythmic patterns and dynamic compositions of *Kathak* are a testament to its rich heritage and cultural significance. The intricate footwork, characterized by swift spins and complex rhythms, is a hallmark of the dance form, requiring both physical agility and mental acuity. Through their movements, *Kathak* dancers weave a tapestry of emotion and expression, conveying stories of romance, heroism, and spiritual devotion.

At the heart of *Kathak* lies the concept of storytelling, with dancers using their bodies as a medium to narrate tales of myth, legend, and folklore. Whether depicting the playful antics of Lord *Krishna* or the eternal love story of *Radha* and *Krishna*, *Kathak* dancers bring these narratives to life with a depth and authenticity that captivates audiences.

But *Kathak* is more than just a dance form; it is a living tradition, a vibrant celebration of culture and heritage that continues to evolve and adapt with the times. In Lucknow, the city of nawabs and poets, *Kathak* finds a fertile ground for artistic expression, with its rich history and cultural legacy serving as a source of inspiration for generations of dancers and musicians.

As we immerse ourselves in the world of *Kathak*, we come to appreciate its timeless beauty and universal appeal. It transcends geographical boundaries and cultural differences, uniting people from all walks of life in a shared appreciation for the arts. In its rhythms and melodies, in its poetry and storytelling, *Kathak* embodies the essence of human creativity and expression, reminding us of the enduring power of art to uplift, inspire, and transform lives.

In the graceful spins and fluid movements of *Kathak*, we see echoes of ancient myths and legends, tales of romance, heroism, and spiritual devotion that have been passed down through generations. The dancers, with their expressive gestures and nuanced expressions, bring these stories to life, captivating audiences with their artistry and grace.

But *Kathak* is more than just a dance form; it is a living tradition, a vibrant celebration of culture and heritage that continues to evolve and adapt with the times. In Lucknow, the city of nawabs and poets, *Kathak* finds a fertile ground for artistic expression, with its rich history and cultural legacy serving as a source of inspiration for generations of dancers and musicians.

As we delve deeper into the world of *Kathak*, we come to appreciate its timeless beauty and universal appeal. It transcends geographical boundaries and cultural differences, uniting people from all walks of life in a shared appreciation for the arts. In its rhythms and melodies, in its poetry and storytelling, *Kathak* embodies the essence of human creativity and expression, reminding us of the enduring power of art to uplift, inspire, and transform lives.

In the graceful spins and fluid movements of *Kathak*, we see echoes of ancient myths and legends, tales of romance, heroism, and spiritual devotion that have been passed down through generations. The dancers, with their expressive gestures and nuanced expressions, bring these stories to life, captivating audiences with their artistry and grace.

But *Kathak* is more than just a dance form; it is a living tradition, a vibrant celebration of culture and heritage that continues to evolve and adapt with the times. In Lucknow, the city of nawabs and poets, *Kathak* finds a fertile ground for artistic expression, with its rich history and cultural legacy serving as a source of inspiration for generations of dancers and musicians.

As we delve deeper into the world of *Kathak*, we come to appreciate its timeless beauty and universal appeal. It transcends geographical boundaries and cultural differences, uniting people from all walks of life in a shared appreciation for the arts. In its rhythms and melodies, in its poetry and storytelling, *Kathak* embodies the essence of human creativity and expression, reminding us of the enduring power of art to uplift, inspire, and transform lives.

As we journey to the eastern state of Odisha, we find ourselves entranced by the ethereal beauty and lyrical movements of *Odissi*, a classical dance form that exudes a profound sense of spirituality and devotion. Originating from the ancient temples of the region, *Odissi* is steeped in centuries of tradition and history, serving as a sacred expression of worship and reverence.

With its fluid movements, graceful poses, and expressive storytelling, Odissi embodies the essence of feminine grace and divine beauty. Each gesture and movement is imbued with symbolic meaning, reflecting the rich tapestry of Odisha's cultural heritage and spiritual beliefs. As we witness the dancers gliding across the stage with effortless elegance, we are transported to a world where time seems to stand still, and the boundaries between the earthly and the divine blur into one.

At the heart of *Odissi* lies a deep connection to mythology and folklore, with dancers portraying the stories of gods and goddesses with unparalleled grace and finesse. Through intricate choreography and emotive expressions, *Odissi* dancers bring these ancient tales to life, exploring themes of love, longing, and the eternal quest for spiritual enlightenment. Each performance is a mesmerizing journey through the realms of myth and legend, captivating audiences with its beauty and depth.

But *Odissi* is more than just a dance form; it is a living tradition, a vibrant celebration of Odisha's rich cultural heritage and spiritual legacy. Passed down through generations, *Odissi* continues to evolve and thrive, adapting to the changing times while remaining true to its roots. In Odisha, the land of temples and traditions, *Odissi* finds a fertile ground for artistic expression, with its sacred sites serving as a constant source of inspiration for dancers and musicians alike.

As we delve deeper into the world of *Odissi*, we come to appreciate its timeless beauty and universal appeal. It transcends language and cultural barriers, touching the hearts and souls of all who witness its mesmerizing performances. In its fluid movements and expressive storytelling, *Odissi* embodies the essence of human emotion and experience, reminding us of the enduring power of art to uplift, inspire, and unite.

In the graceful poses and emotive expressions of *Odissi*, we find echoes of ancient wisdom and spiritual enlightenment, inviting us to contemplate the deeper mysteries of life and existence. Through its divine beauty and profound grace, *Odissi* becomes a window into the soul of Odisha, revealing the timeless truths and eternal values that have shaped its culture and civilization for centuries.

As we immerse ourselves in the world of *Odissi*, we are drawn into a sacred journey of self-discovery and spiritual awakening. With each graceful movement and expressive gesture, we are reminded of the inherent beauty and divinity that resides within us all. *Odissi* becomes not just a dance form but a transformative experience, inviting us to embrace the divine within and connect with the universal essence of existence.

In the eastern state of Odisha, amidst the ancient temples and verdant landscapes, Odissi continues to flourish as a beacon of artistic excellence and spiritual enlightenment. Through its timeless beauty and profound grace, it inspires generations of artists and enthusiasts to seek deeper meaning and purpose in their lives, forging a connection to the divine that transcends the boundaries of time and space.

As we delve deeper into the rich musical traditions of India, we discover a kaleidoscope of genres and styles that reflect the country's diverse cultural heritage. From the soulful melodies of Hindustani classical music to the rhythmic beats of folk and tribal music, each genre is a unique expression of regional identity and artistic innovation. With its intricate *ragas*, *talas*, and improvisational techniques, Indian classical music is a testament to the profound connection between music, spirituality, and human emotion.

As we find ourselves wandering through the vibrant streets of Mumbai, the beating heart of India's entertainment industry, we are immediately engulfed in the pulsating rhythms and infectious energy of Bollywood music and dance. Here, amidst the bustling crowds and cacophony of sounds, Bollywood reigns supreme, its larger-than-life presence permeating every corner of the city.

Born out of the dynamic fusion of traditional Indian music with Western influences, Bollywood has evolved into a global phenomenon, captivating audiences far and wide with its unique blend of colourful choreography, catchy tunes, and melodramatic storytelling. What began as a local entertainment industry has now transcended geographical boundaries, finding resonance with diverse audiences across continents.

In the world of Bollywood, music and dance are not merely forms of entertainment; they are powerful expressions of emotion, identity, and cultural heritage. Through its vibrant song and dance sequences, Bollywood celebrates the joy of life, the power of love, and the resilience of the human spirit. Each dance move, each musical note, carries with it a story – a tale of romance, triumph, or redemption that resonates deeply with audiences of all ages and backgrounds.

The choreography of Bollywood dance sequences is as diverse as the country itself, drawing inspiration from classical Indian dance forms, folk traditions, and contemporary styles. From the graceful movements of *Kathak* to the energetic beats of *Bhangra*, Bollywood choreography is a kaleidoscope of colour and movement, reflecting the rich cultural tapestry of India.

But it's not just the choreography that makes Bollywood dance so captivating; it's the infectious energy and enthusiasm of the performers that truly bring the magic to life. Whether it's the graceful expressions of a leading actress or the energetic moves of a group of background dancers, there's an undeniable sense of joy and passion that radiates from every performance.

In the world of Bollywood, music and dance are not just forms of entertainment; they are a way of life. They have the power to uplift spirits, ignite imaginations, and bring people together in a shared experience of joy and celebration. Whether it's a lavish dance number set against the backdrop of the Swiss Alps or a lively street dance sequence shot in the narrow lanes of Mumbai, Bollywood transports audiences to a world of fantasy and escapism, where anything is possible and dreams can come true.

But perhaps the most remarkable thing about Bollywood is its ability to transcend cultural boundaries and unite people from all walks of life in a shared appreciation for music and dance. Whether you're in Mumbai or Manhattan, London or Lahore, the infectious beats of a Bollywood song have the power to make you tap your feet and sway to the rhythm, forging connections that defy language, nationality, and creed.

In a world often divided by differences, Bollywood serves as a powerful reminder of our shared humanity, our common love for music, and our innate desire to express ourselves through movement and rhythm. It reminds us that, no matter where we come from or what language we speak, we can all find common ground on the dance floor, where the universal language of music brings us together in harmony and joy.

As we embark on a journey through the rich musical traditions and classical dance forms of India, we are immediately struck by the depth and diversity of artistic expression that permeates every aspect of these ancient art forms. From the rhythmic beats of classical tabla compositions to the graceful movements of Bharatanatyam dancers, Indian music and dance serve as profound reflections of life, culture, and spirituality.

At the heart of Indian music and dance lies a deep reverence for tradition and heritage, with each performance serving as a homage to the centuries-old rituals and practices that have been passed down through generations. Whether it's the soul-stirring melodies of Hindustani classical music or the intricate footwork of Kathak dancers, there is an undeniable sense of connection to the past, a recognition of the timeless beauty and wisdom that transcends the boundaries of time and space.

But Indian music and dance are not merely relics of the past; they are living traditions that continue to evolve and adapt with the times. In today's fast-paced world, where technology and globalization have reshaped the cultural landscape, Indian artists are finding new ways to innovate and experiment while staying true to their roots. From fusion music collaborations to contemporary reinterpretations of classical dance forms, Indian artists are pushing the boundaries of creativity and cultural expression, ushering in a new era of artistic excellence and innovation.

Through their rhythmic cadences, graceful movements, and emotive storytelling, Indian music and dance have the power to inspire, uplift, and enchant audiences around the world. Whether it's the haunting strains of a classical *raga* or the dynamic rhythms of a Bollywood dance number, Indian artists have a unique ability to evoke a wide range of emotions and experiences, transporting listeners and viewers to realms of beauty and wonder.

One of the most remarkable aspects of Indian music and dance is their ability to serve as a bridge between the past and the present, the traditional and the modern. In a rapidly changing world, where cultural heritage is often overshadowed by the demands of progress and development, Indian artists are playing a vital role in preserving and promoting the rich legacy of their ancestors while also embracing the opportunities of the digital age. Indian music is a multifaceted and dynamic art form that continues to evolve and adapt with the times while remaining true to its ancient roots. Its emphasis on improvisation, spirituality, and intricate rhythm makes it a truly unique and captivating musical tradition that continues to inspire and enchant audiences around the world.

In the age of globalization, Indian music and dance have emerged as powerful ambassadors of culture and identity, transcending geographical boundaries and linguistic barriers to connect people from all walks of life in a shared celebration of artistic excellence and cultural diversity. Whether it's a classical concert in New York City or a Bollywood dance workshop in Tokyo, Indian artists are finding new audiences and spreading the magic of their art forms to every corner of the globe.

But perhaps the most enduring legacy of Indian music and dance is their ability to inspire and uplift the human spirit. In a world often filled with chaos and uncertainty, these ancient art forms serve as beacons of hope and light, reminding us of the beauty and wonder that surrounds us and the power of creativity to transcend the limitations of the human experience.

In the end, Indian music and dance are more than just artistic expressions; they are a celebration of life itself, a testament to the enduring power of creativity and cultural expression. Through their rhythmic cadences, graceful movements, and emotive storytelling, they continue to inspire, uplift, and enchant audiences around the world, weaving together the threads of tradition and innovation to create a vibrant tapestry of cultural heritage and artistic excellence that will endure for generations to come.

CHAPTER VII

Sacred Spaces

Our journey through India's sacred spaces begins with a sense of reverence and anticipation, as we shed the roles of mere tourists and embrace the deeper significance of our pilgrimage. With each step, we feel a connection to the countless generations of devotees who have walked these paths before us, their prayers and aspirations echoing through the corridors of time.

As we approach these architectural marvels, we are struck not only by their physical beauty but also by the spiritual energy that permeates their surroundings. Whether it's the towering spires of a temple, the elegant arches of a mosque, or the serene simplicity of a church, each sacred space seems to radiate a sense of divine presence, inviting us to pause, reflect, and connect with something greater than ourselves.

In the ancient city of Varanasi, where the sacred Ganges flows like a river of eternity, we are drawn to the *Kashi Vishwanath Temple*, a timeless symbol of devotion and faith. As we stand before its majestic entrance, we are enveloped in the fragrance of incense and the soft glow of oil lamps, transported to a realm where the material world fades away, and only the eternal truths of the soul remain.

In the bustling streets of Delhi, amidst the chaos of urban life, we find solace and serenity in the grandeur of the *Jama Masjid*, a testament to the enduring legacy of Islamic architecture. Here, amidst the call to prayer and the hum of human activity, we find a moment of stillness and contemplation, as if the noise of the world were silenced by the timeless beauty of this sacred space.

Traveling southwards to the coastal city of Kochi, we are captivated by the St. Francis Church, a silent witness to the ebb and flow of history. Here, amidst the whispering palms and the salt-tinged air, we find ourselves surrounded by the echoes of centuries past, as if the ghosts of the colonial era were whispering secrets in our ears.

Venturing into the verdant hills of Amritsar, we are humbled by the resplendent Golden Temple, a beacon of hope and compassion in a world often darkened by division and strife. Here, amidst the shimmering waters of the *Amrit Sarovar,* we find ourselves bathed in the golden light of divine grace, our hearts uplifted by the spirit of unity and brotherhood that pervades this sacred space.

From the snow-capped peaks of the Himalayas to the sun-drenched shores of the Indian Ocean, India's sacred spaces are as diverse and varied as the country itself. Each temple, mosque, church, and *gurudwara* is a testament to the enduring power of faith and the universal human longing for transcendence and connection. As we journey through these sacred sites, we are reminded of the profound truth that lies at the heart of all religions, amid life's joys and sorrows, there is a divine presence that guides and sustains us, offering solace, hope, and eternal peace.

In the ancient city of Varanasi, where time seems to stand still amidst the eternal flow of the Ganges River, the *Kashi Vishwanath* Temple stands as a sacred sentinel, beckoning pilgrims from far and wide to its hallowed precincts. This temple, dedicated to Lord *Shiva,* the Supreme according to the Hindu Holy Scriptures, holds a revered place in the hearts of devotees, serving as a beacon of divine light amidst the tumultuous currents of earthly existence.

As we approach the temple, we are immediately struck by its majestic presence, with towering spires that seem to reach towards the heavens themselves. These spires, adorned with intricate carvings and sacred symbols, symbolize the eternal quest for spiritual enlightenment, reminding us of the timeless truths that lie beyond the realm of material existence.

Stepping through the ornately carved entrance, we are enveloped in a world of beauty and wonder, where every stone tells a story and every sculpture speaks of divine grace. The walls of the temple are adorned with images of gods and goddesses, each representing a different aspect of the divine, from the compassionate goddess *Parvati* to the fierce warrior deity *Mahakala*.

As we wander through the temple's sacred halls, we are greeted by the reverent chants of devotees and the rhythmic clang of temple bells, creating a symphony of sound that reverberates through the very core of our being. Here, amidst the hustle and bustle of everyday life, we find a sanctuary of peace and tranquility, where the chaos of the world fades away and only the eternal presence of the divine remains.

But perhaps the most profound experience of all is the *darshan*, or divine sight, of the deity himself. As we stand before the sanctum sanctorum, where the sacred lingam of Lord *Shiva* resides, we are filled with a sense of awe and reverence unlike anything we have ever known. At that moment, we feel a profound sense of connection to the divine, as if the very essence of the universe were pulsating within these ancient walls, reminding us of our divine nature and the eternal bond that unites us all.

In the sacred city of Varanasi, where the ancient and the eternal converge, the Kashi Vishwanath Temple stands as a testament to the enduring power of faith and the timeless wisdom of the divine. Here, amidst the swirling currents of the Ganges River and the ceaseless flow of human existence, we find solace, hope, and eternal peace, as we journey ever closer to the heart of the divine. Traveling southwards to the coastal city of Kochi, we are transported back in time to the era of European colonialism, where the St. Francis Church stands as a silent witness to the ebb and flow of history. Built by Portuguese settlers in the early 16th century, the church is a testament to the enduring power of faith amidst the turmoil of conquest and colonization. Its simple yet elegant facade speaks volumes about the resilience of the human spirit as if to say that no matter how dark the night may seem, the light of faith will always shine through. As we wander through its quiet halls and sunlit courtyards, we are reminded of the timeless truths that unite us all, the universal longing for love, compassion, and spiritual fulfillment.

In the bustling streets of Delhi, where the rhythm of life pulses with the vibrancy of India's cultural heritage, the Jama Masjid stands as a majestic testament to the enduring legacy of Islamic architecture. Constructed in the 17th century under the patronage of Emperor Shah Jahan, this magnificent mosque is a quintessential example of Mughal design, captivating the senses with its towering minarets, grand courtyard, and exquisite marble domes.

Approaching the Jama Masjid, we are immediately struck by its imposing presence, the intricacy of its architectural details hinting at the grandeur that lies within. As we step through the intricately adorned gateway and into the vast courtyard beyond, we are enveloped in a sense of tranquility and serenity that belies the bustling energy of the city beyond its walls. It is as though time itself slows down within these sacred precincts, allowing us to escape the frenetic pace of modern life and find respite in the contemplative embrace of divine grace.

The Jama Masjid's grand courtyard, with its expansive marble floor and symmetrical layout, exudes a sense of harmony and balance that speaks to the inherent order of the universe. Here, amidst the gentle rustle of palm leaves and the soothing trickle of water from ornate fountains, we find ourselves drawn into a state of inner peace and reflection, as if the chaos of the outside world were held at bay by the sheer force of spiritual tranquility.

As we gaze up at the mosque's towering minarets, soaring towards the heavens like pillars of faith, we are reminded of the timeless beauty and resilience of the human spirit. Each minaret stands as a symbol of devotion and dedication, a testament to the enduring power of faith to uplift and inspire the soul. As we marvel at the intricate details of the mosque's marble domes, adorned with delicate arabesque patterns and calligraphic inscriptions, we are reminded of the profound artistry and craftsmanship that went into its creation.

Inside the mosque, the air is alive with the soft murmur of prayers and the scent of fragrant incense, creating a sensory tapestry that heightens our spiritual experience. Here, amidst the warm glow of sunlight filtering through stained glass windows and the soft glow of candlelight, we find solace and peace in the presence of the divine, as if all the worries and troubles of the world had vanished in the light of eternal truth.

In the Jama Masjid, amidst the prayers of the faithful and the scent of fragrant incense, we discover a sanctuary of peace and serenity, where the chaos of the outside world fades away and only the timeless presence of the divine remains. It is a place where hearts are uplifted, spirits renewed, and souls touched by the gentle hand of grace, reminding us of the eternal truths that bind us all together in the tapestry of human experience.

Venturing into the lush green hills of Amritsar, where the air is imbued with a sense of sanctity and serenity, we are greeted by the majestic sight of the resplendent Golden Temple. This iconic shrine, revered as the holiest site in Sikhism, stands as a beacon of spiritual enlightenment and communal harmony, drawing pilgrims and visitors from all corners of the globe.

As we approach the Golden Temple, our eyes are immediately drawn to its shimmering golden domes, which seem to glow with an ethereal radiance in the sunlight. The temple's architecture is a testament to the rich heritage of Sikh culture, with its intricate marble facades, ornate gilded embellishments, and graceful archways that speak of a bygone era of artistic grandeur.

Surrounded by the tranquil waters of the *Amrit Sarovar*, or Pool of Nectar, the Golden Temple appears to float serenely amidst a sea of tranquility. The sacred pool, whose waters are believed to possess healing properties, serves as a spiritual oasis for pilgrims seeking solace and renewal, their reflections mirroring the timeless beauty of the temple above.

As we step through the imposing entrance gates and into the temple complex, we are greeted by the melodious strains of sacred hymns, or kirtans, which fill the air with a sense of divine harmony and devotion. The sound of the hymns, accompanied by the rhythmic beat of drums and the lilting melody of flutes, transports us to a realm of spiritual ecstasy, where the boundaries between the material and the divine dissolve in a symphony of devotion.

Amidst the throngs of pilgrims and devotees who have come to pay homage to the Guru Granth Sahib, the holy scripture of Sikhism, we feel a profound sense of unity and brotherhood that transcends the barriers of language, culture, and creed. Here, in the sacred precincts of the Golden Temple, people of all faiths are welcomed with open arms, their hearts united in a shared experience of love, compassion, and service.

As we join the community in partaking of the *langar* or communal meal, we are reminded of the power of compassion and service to nourish not only the body but also the soul. Sitting side by side with strangers from distant lands, we share in the simple yet profound act of breaking bread together, our differences melting away in the warmth of shared humanity.

In the Golden Temple, amidst the throngs of pilgrims and the sound of sacred hymns, we find a sanctuary of peace and harmony, where the divine presence is palpable and the spirit of brotherhood reigns supreme. It is a place where hearts are uplifted, souls are nourished, and the eternal truths of love and compassion are made manifest in every act of service and devotion.

From the majestic mountains of the Himalayas to the serene shores of the Indian Ocean, India's sacred spaces form a kaleidoscope of spiritual diversity, each one a reflection of the country's rich tapestry of faiths, cultures, and traditions. As we traverse this sacred landscape, we are struck by the sheer breadth and depth of religious expression, from the ancient rituals of Hinduism to the solemn prayers of Islam, the solemn hymns of Christianity, and the meditative chants of Sikhism.

In the foothills of the Himalayas, where the air is crisp with the scent of pine and the sound of rushing rivers, we find ourselves standing before ancient temples dedicated to the gods and goddesses of Hindu mythology. Here, amidst the echoing chants of priests and the fragrance of incense, we are transported to a realm where time seems to stand still, and the divine presence feels palpable in the very air we breathe.

In the heart of bustling cities like Delhi and Mumbai, we encounter the majestic mosques and towering minarets of Islam, where the faithful gather to offer their prayers and seek solace in the words of the Quran. Here, amidst the hustle and bustle of urban life, we find moments of stillness and reflection, as the call to prayer echoes through the crowded streets, reminding us of the timeless truths that unite us all.

In the tranquil countryside of Kerala and Goa, we discover the humble chapels and ornate cathedrals of Christianity, where the faithful gather to celebrate the life and teachings of Jesus Christ. Here, amidst the flickering candlelight and the haunting strains of hymns, we are reminded of the power of faith to transcend boundaries and transform lives, offering hope and redemption to all who seek it.

And in the vibrant cities of Punjab and Gujarat, we are welcomed into the gurdwaras of Sikhism, where the sound of *Gurbani* fills the air with a sense of peace and serenity. Here, amidst the communal kitchens and the shared meals of langar, we experience the true essence of Sikhism, the belief in the equality of all people and the importance of service to others.

As we journey through the hallowed grounds of India's sacred sites, we are enveloped in a profound sense of reverence and awe, for we recognize that beyond the physical structures and religious rituals lies a deeper truth that resonates with the very essence of our being. It is the recognition that amidst the ebb and flow of life's myriad experiences, be it moments of joy and celebration or times of sorrow and despair, there exists a divine presence, a guiding force that transcends the limitations of human understanding and offers solace, hope, and eternal peace.

Amid bustling cities and serene countryside, amidst the clamor of daily life and the quiet solitude of contemplation, we encounter this divine presence in myriad forms, whether it be through the solemn chants of priests, the melodious recitations of holy scriptures, or the whispered prayers of devotees seeking solace in times of need. It is a presence that knows no bounds, transcending the barriers of language, culture, and creed, and embracing all who seek its comfort and guidance.

As we stand before ancient temples, majestic mosques, ornate churches, and humble gurdwaras, we are reminded of the universal truths that lie at the heart of all religions, the belief in a higher power that watches over us, the understanding that we are all interconnected as part of a larger tapestry of creation, and the recognition that love, compassion, and service are the cornerstones of a life well-lived.

In the sacred spaces of India, where the divine meets the earthly and the mundane merges with the transcendent, we find ourselves drawn into a deeper understanding of our shared humanity and the interconnectedness of all living beings. It is a realization that each of us, regardless of our background or beliefs, is bound together by the common thread of existence and that in embracing this interconnectedness, we find strength, solace, and hope for the journey ahead.

As we journey through these sacred sites, we are reminded not only of the profound truths that lie at the heart of all religions but also of our capacity to connect with the divine within ourselves and each other. It is a journey of self-discovery and spiritual awakening, a pilgrimage of the soul that leads us closer to the eternal truth that lies at the core of our being, that amidst life's joys and sorrows, there is a divine presence that guides and sustains us, offering solace, hope, and eternal peace.

CHAPTER VIII

The Language and Literature of India

As you traverse the vast expanse of India's cultural landscape, you become increasingly aware of the intricate interplay between language and literature, which emerges as a fundamental aspect of the nation's identity. This journey through India is akin to a voyage through time and space, where every corner reveals new layers of linguistic diversity and literary richness.

Imagine yourself standing at the foothills of the majestic Himalayas, where the air is crisp and the landscape awe-inspiring. Here, amidst the towering peaks and verdant valleys, you encounter a tapestry of languages that mirror the diversity of the region's geography. From the lilting melodies of Garhwali in Uttarakhand to the robust dialects of Himachali in Himachal Pradesh, each linguistic variant carries within it the stories of the land and its people, echoing through the ages like whispers in the wind.

As you journey southward, the landscape undergoes a dramatic transformation, giving way to the lush greenery and tranquil waters of Kerala's backwaters. Here, amidst the coconut groves and emerald rice paddies, the language takes on a lyrical quality, reminiscent of the rhythms of nature itself. Malayalam, with its rich literary tradition dating back centuries, becomes a vehicle for poetic expression, weaving tales of love, longing, and the eternal cycle of life and death.

In the bustling cities of Mumbai, Kolkata, and Chennai, you are confronted with a cacophony of languages and dialects, each vying for attention in the vibrant tapestry of urban life. In Mumbai, the cosmopolitan hub of India, the streets resound with the cadence of Marathi, Gujarati, Hindi, and English, reflecting the city's melting pot of cultures and communities. In Kolkata, the cultural capital of the country, Bengali takes center stage, its mellifluous tones infusing the air with a sense of poetry and passion. And in Chennai, the heart of Tamil Nadu, the melodious strains of Tamil fill the streets, embodying the region's rich literary and cultural heritage.

But it is not just the spoken word that defines India's linguistic landscape; it is also the written word, enshrined in the annals of its literary tradition. From the ancient epics of the Ramayana and Mahabharata to the modern works of contemporary authors, Indian literature spans a vast spectrum of genres, styles, and themes. In the works of luminaries such as Rabindranath Tagore, Salman Rushdie, and Arundhati Roy, you find reflections of India's complex and multifaceted society, grappling with issues of identity, inequality, and social justice.

As you immerse yourself in the rich tapestry of Indian language and literature, you come to realize that it is not just a means of communication or artistic expression; it is a living testament to the resilience, creativity, and diversity of the Indian people. It is a mirror that reflects the soul of a nation, a nation that celebrates its differences even as it seeks to find common ground in the shared experience of being Indian. It is through this celebration of language and literature that India continues to inspire and captivate, inviting all who encounter it to embark on a journey of discovery and enlightenment.

India's linguistic diversity is a testament to the nation's rich cultural tapestry, where each language and dialect is a thread weaving together the intricate fabric of its identity.

Imagine wandering through the labyrinthine streets of Mumbai, India's bustling metropolis, and the beating heart of the Hindi film industry, where the cadence of Marathi reverberates alongside the rhythmic beats of Bollywood music. Here, amidst the chaos of the city, the vibrant hues of Marathi culture paint a vivid picture of resilience and vitality, reflecting the indomitable spirit of its people.

Journeying further north, you find yourself amidst the verdant fields of Punjab, where the lyrical Punjabi script adorns signs and billboards, infusing the landscape with a sense of pride and belonging. In Punjab, language is more than just a means of communication; it is a symbol of cultural identity and heritage, passed down through generations with reverence and affection. From the rustic charm of Punjabi folk songs to the exuberance of Bhangra dance, the spirit of Punjab finds expression in its language and traditions, celebrating the joy of life and the warmth of community.

Venturing into the remote corners of Arunachal Pradesh, nestled amidst the pristine beauty of the Himalayas, you encounter a linguistic landscape as diverse and awe-inspiring as the natural surroundings. Here, amidst the snow-capped peaks and dense forests, dozens of indigenous languages and dialects flourish, each with its unique sounds and symbols, reflecting the ancient customs and traditions of its people. In this remote corner of India, language is not just a means of communication; it is a lifeline connecting communities across vast distances, preserving cultural heritage, and fostering a sense of belonging in a rapidly changing world.

In the bustling urban sprawl of Delhi, India's bustling capital city, you witness the convergence of cultures and languages from across the country. Here, amidst the cacophony of honking horns and bustling marketplaces, the linguistic mosaic of India's diversity comes alive, as speakers of Hindi, Urdu, English, and myriad regional languages mingle and interact. In Delhi, language serves as a bridge that connects people from all walks of life, transcending barriers of geography, religion, and social class, and fostering a sense of unity in diversity that is quintessentially Indian.

At the heart of India's linguistic diversity lies a deep sense of pride and belonging, where each language and dialect is cherished as a unique expression of the country's rich cultural heritage. From the bustling streets of Mumbai to the remote corners of Arunachal Pradesh, language serves as a powerful symbol of identity and community, uniting people across vast distances and fostering a sense of belonging in an ever-changing world.

Delving deeper into the rich tapestry of Indian literature is akin to embarking on a journey through time itself, where each page reveals new layers of wisdom, insight, and inspiration. At the very foundation of this literary tradition lie the ancient Sanskrit epics of the Ramayana and Mahabharata, monumental works that have stood the test of time to become timeless pillars of wisdom and morality. These epics, steeped in myth and legend, offer profound insights into the human condition, exploring themes of love, duty, honor, and the eternal struggle between good and evil.

As you immerse yourself in the epic narratives of the Ramayana and Mahabharata, you are transported to a world of gods and goddesses, heroes and villains, whose deeds and destinies shape the course of history and the fate of humanity. Here, amidst the celestial battles and epic quests, you encounter timeless truths and universal principles that resonate across cultures and civilizations, offering guidance and solace to generations of readers.

But Indian literature is not confined to the grandeur of epic poetry; it also encompasses a wealth of mystical and spiritual writings that transcend religious divides and speak to the depths of the human soul. In the mystical verses of the Sufi saints, you discover a profound sense of unity and interconnectedness that transcends the boundaries of faith and belief. Through their poetry, the Sufi mystics offer glimpses into the ineffable mysteries of existence, inviting readers to embark on a journey of self-discovery and spiritual awakening.

These literary masterpieces passed down through generations via oral tradition and written manuscripts, serve as guiding beacons illuminating the path of truth, righteousness, and enlightenment. In the words of the ancient sages and wise poets, you find echoes of timeless wisdom and profound insight, guiding you on your quest for meaning and understanding. Whether through the epic narratives of the Ramayana and Mahabharata or the mystical verses of the Sufi saints, Indian literature offers a treasure trove of literary gems that continue to inspire, uplift, and enlighten readers around the world.

In the vibrant bazaars and bustling bookshops that dot India's landscape, you are enveloped in a kaleidoscope of literary treasures that capture the very essence of Indian life and society. Here, amidst the hustle and bustle of everyday life, you encounter a diverse array of literary works that serve as windows into the rich tapestry of Indian culture, offering insights into the hopes, dreams, struggles, and triumphs of its people.

One such literary luminary whose works resonate deeply with readers is Munshi Premchand, often regarded as one of the foremost figures in Hindi literature. Through his poignant prose and compassionate storytelling, Premchand delves into the lives of ordinary people, illuminating the complexities of human existence with empathy and insight. His stories, set against the backdrop of rural India, explore themes of social injustice, poverty, and the indomitable human spirit, striking a chord with readers across generations.

In the realm of poetry, Rabindranath Tagore stands as an iconic figure whose lyrical verses continue to captivate hearts and minds around the world. Tagore's poetry, infused with a deep sense of spirituality and reverence for nature, evokes the beauty and majesty of the natural world, inviting readers to contemplate the mysteries of existence and the interconnectedness of all living beings. Through his timeless verses, Tagore celebrates the universal themes of love, longing, and the search for meaning, transcending the boundaries of language and culture to touch the very soul of humanity.

But Indian literature is not confined to the works of these literary giants alone; it encompasses a vast and diverse range of voices and perspectives that collectively paint a vivid portrait of Indian society. From the stirring tales of R.K. Narayan, whose novels transport readers to the idyllic streets of Malgudi, to the incisive satire of Arundhati Roy, whose writing explores the complexities of contemporary India, Indian literature reflects the myriad hues of the nation's cultural and social landscape.

In the pages of Indian literature, you find echoes of the past, reflections of the present, and visions of the future, woven together in a rich tapestry of words and ideas. It is a literature that celebrates the human experience in all its complexity and diversity, offering solace, inspiration, and a deeper understanding of the world we inhabit. As you immerse yourself in the literary treasures of India, you cannot help but marvel at the profound wisdom and timeless beauty contained within its pages.

Among the luminaries of Indian literature, you encounter towering figures whose contributions have left an indelible mark on the cultural fabric of the nation. They are the literary giants whose words have echoed through the corridors of time, shaping the collective consciousness of generations and offering profound insights into the human condition.

At the forefront of this pantheon stands Rabindranath Tagore, the visionary poet, playwright, and philosopher whose works transcend the boundaries of language and culture. Tagore's poetry, imbued with a profound sense of spirituality and reverence for nature, continues to inspire readers around the world with its timeless beauty and universal themes. Through his evocative verses, Tagore captures the essence of the human experience, exploring themes of love, longing, and the quest for spiritual enlightenment.

Alongside Tagore, Mulk Raj Anand emerges as a towering figure whose novels serve as powerful indictments of social injustice and inequality. Anand's incisive social commentary exposes the harsh realities of colonialism and caste oppression, shining a light on the plight of the marginalized and disenfranchised in Indian society. Through his works such as "Untouchable" and "Coolie," Anand challenges readers to confront uncomfortable truths and imagine a more just and equitable world.

In the realm of modern Indian literature, Arundhati Roy stands as a beacon of literary excellence, whose novels blend incisive political critique with lyrical prose and vivid imagery. Roy's debut novel, "The God of Small Things," won the prestigious Booker Prize and catapulted her to international acclaim. Since then, Roy has continued to push the boundaries of literary convention, using her platform to advocate for social justice, environmental conservation, and human rights.

But the legacy of Indian literature extends far beyond these individual luminaries; it encompasses a vast and diverse array of voices and perspectives that collectively paint a vibrant portrait of Indian society. From the stirring poetry of Sarojini Naidu to the groundbreaking fiction of Salman Rushdie, Indian authors and poets have wielded their pens as instruments of change and transformation, challenging conventions, and reshaping the literary landscape.

In the pages of Indian literature, you find not only stories and poems but also reflections on the hopes, dreams, struggles, and triumphs of a nation. It is a literature that celebrates the richness and diversity of Indian culture, while also confronting its complexities and contradictions. As you immerse yourself in the works of these literary luminaries, you cannot help but be moved by the power of their words to illuminate, inspire, and provoke thought.

But beyond the celebrated authors and poets lie countless untold stories and voices waiting to be heard. These are the voices of ordinary people whose experiences and perspectives have been woven into the fabric of India's rich tapestry of oral and written traditions. In the remote villages of Rajasthan, you listen to the age-old ballads of the bards, whose oral traditions have preserved the folklore and legends of bygone eras. These ballads passed down from generation to generation, offer a glimpse into the cultural heritage and collective memory of the region, celebrating the triumphs and tragedies of its people in lyrical verse.

In the bustling metropolises of Kolkata and Chennai, you encounter the vibrant voices of young writers and poets, whose words reflect the zeitgeist of contemporary India. These are the voices of a new generation, grappling with issues of identity, globalization, and social change in a rapidly evolving society. Through their poetry and prose, they explore themes of love, loss, longing, and belonging, offering fresh perspectives on age-old questions and challenging the status quo with their bold and innovative storytelling.

In the pages of their works, you find echoes of your own experiences and struggles, as well as glimpses of a future yet to unfold. These are the voices that breathe life into the characters and landscapes of Indian literature, infusing them with authenticity, depth, and resonance. And as you listen to their stories and poems, you realize that Indian literature is not just a reflection of the past or present, but a living, breathing testament to the resilience, creativity, and diversity of the human spirit.

As you navigate the labyrinth of Indian language and literature, you are struck by the profound truth that lies at its core, the power of words to transcend barriers of time and space, to bridge divides and foster understanding, and to capture the essence of the human spirit in all its complexity and diversity. In the pages of India's literary canon, you find not just stories and poems but mirrors reflecting the soul of a nation, a nation whose linguistic diversity and literary heritage continue to inspire and captivate, generation after generation.

Indian language and literature are more than mere tools of communication; they are vessels of culture, repositories of history, and embodiments of identity. From the ancient Sanskrit texts to the modern works of contemporary authors, each word carries with it the weight of centuries of tradition and innovation, of struggle and resilience, of joy and sorrow. In the eloquent verses of Kalidasa and the stirring prose of Premchand, you find echoes of the past and glimpses of the future, intertwined in a timeless dance of creativity and expression.

But Indian language and literature are not static entities confined to the pages of books; they are living, breathing entities that evolve and adapt with the passage of time. In the bustling streets of Mumbai and the remote villages of Assam, you encounter the vibrant tapestry of linguistic diversity that characterizes India's cultural landscape. Here, amidst the cacophony of languages and dialects, each word spoken is a testament to the richness and resilience of India's linguistic heritage, a reminder of the power of language to shape our understanding of the world and ourselves.

In the pages of India's literary canon, you find stories of triumph and tragedy, of love and loss, of courage and sacrifice. These are stories that transcend the boundaries of time and space, resonating with readers across generations and cultures. They are stories that capture the human experience in all its complexity and diversity, offering insights into the universal truths that bind us together as members of the human family.

As you immerse yourself in the world of Indian language and literature, you embark on a journey of discovery, where each page turned is a revelation, each word a revelation. In this vast and diverse landscape of literary treasures, you encounter the stirring verses of Rabindranath Tagore, whose poetry transports you to ethereal realms of beauty and truth. Through his words, you feel the gentle caress of the wind, the warmth of the sun, and the eternal dance of life and death.

But the world of Indian language and literature is not confined to the works of Tagore alone; it is a vibrant tapestry woven with the threads of countless voices and perspectives. From the thought-provoking essays of Arundhati Roy to the poignant stories of R.K. Narayan, Indian literature offers a kaleidoscope of experiences and insights, each one a testament to the richness and diversity of Indian culture.

As you journey through the pages of India's literary landscape, you are struck by the profound truth that lies at its core, that words have the power to inspire, provoke, and transform. Whether through the lyrical verses of ancient Sanskrit texts or the contemporary prose of modern-day authors, Indian language and literature offer a window into the soul of a nation, a soul that is as diverse and vibrant as the languages and cultures that comprise it.

And as you delve deeper into this world of words and ideas, you come to realize that literature is not just a mirror reflecting the world around us, but a catalyst for change, a force that can shape hearts and minds, challenge conventions, and ignite revolutions. In the hands of gifted writers and poets, words become weapons of resistance, tools for social justice, and beacons of hope in a world filled with darkness.

So, as you journey through the pages of India's literary landscape, remember the profound truth that lies at its core, that words have the power to change the world, one story at a time. And may you continue to be inspired, provoked, and transformed by the magic of Indian language and literature, as you navigate the ever-changing currents of life and thought.

CHAPTER IX

Traditional Medicine and Healing Practices

The ancient healing traditions of India, deeply woven into the fabric of its cultural heritage, serve as guiding lights illuminating the path to holistic well-being. Within the intricate tapestry of Ayurveda, Yoga, and traditional herbal remedies, lies a profound understanding of the interconnectedness between the physical, mental, and spiritual aspects of human existence.

Ayurveda, often revered as the "science of life," is a time-honored healing system that finds its roots in the ancient scriptures known as the Vedas. At its core, Ayurveda recognizes that each individual is a unique manifestation of the five elements, earth, water, fire, air, and ether, and that optimal health is achieved through harmony and balance within these elemental forces. Through personalized assessments based on one's dosha constitution, Vata, Pitta, and Kapha, Ayurveda offers tailored recommendations encompassing diet, lifestyle, herbal remedies, and therapeutic practices to restore equilibrium and promote vitality.

Complementing Ayurveda is the timeless practice of Yoga, a profound spiritual discipline that seeks to unify the body, mind, and spirit. Through the practice of asanas (physical postures), pranayama (breath control), and meditation, Yoga cultivates awareness, strength, and flexibility on both physical and mental levels. By harnessing the power of breath and movement, Yoga serves as a gateway to inner peace, self-discovery, and spiritual awakening, fostering a deep sense of connection with oneself and the world around.

In tandem with Ayurveda and Yoga, traditional herbal remedies form an integral part of India's holistic approach to health and wellness. Drawing upon the rich botanical bounty of the Indian subcontinent, traditional healers have long relied on the healing properties of herbs, roots, and spices to address a myriad of health concerns. From the immune-boosting effects of tulsi (holy basil) to the digestive support provided by ginger and turmeric, these natural remedies offer gentle yet potent solutions that align with the body's innate healing intelligence.

Together, Ayurveda, Yoga, and traditional herbal remedies embody a holistic paradigm of health and wellness that acknowledges the interconnectedness of all aspects of being, physical, mental, emotional, and spiritual. Rooted in ancient wisdom yet relevant in the modern world, these time-tested practices offer a roadmap to vibrant health, inner harmony, and radiant living.

As we journey deeper into the timeless tapestry of India's healing traditions, let us embrace the wisdom of the past and the promise of the future, as we embark on a transformative journey of self-discovery, healing, and wholeness. May the ancient teachings of Ayurveda, Yoga, and traditional herbal medicine continue to inspire and empower us to live our lives in alignment with the natural rhythms of the universe, cultivating health, happiness, and well-being for ourselves and all beings.

Ayurveda, often revered as the "science of life," represents an intricate tapestry of ancient wisdom that has been meticulously woven into the cultural fabric of India for millennia. Its roots can be traced back to the sacred texts of the Vedas, the oldest scriptures of Hindu philosophy and knowledge, where its foundational principles were first articulated. Over the centuries, Ayurveda has been nurtured and refined by generations of sages, scholars, and healers across the Indian subcontinent, evolving into a comprehensive system of holistic healing that continues to resonate with seekers of wellness around the world.

At the heart of Ayurveda lies a profound understanding of the inherent uniqueness of each individual. According to Ayurvedic philosophy, every person is born with a distinctive constitution, known as Prakriti, which determines their physical, mental, and emotional characteristics. This constitution is influenced by a complex interplay of the five elements, earth, water, fire, air, and ether, as well as the three doshas: Vata, Pitta, and Kapha. These doshas represent the dynamic forces of nature that govern all biological processes within the body, regulating everything from metabolism and digestion to mood and temperament.

Through a personalized approach to healing, Ayurveda seeks to restore balance and harmony to the doshas, thereby promoting optimal health and vitality. This involves identifying the unique constitution and imbalances of each individual through a comprehensive assessment of physical symptoms, lifestyle factors, and psychological tendencies. Based on this assessment, Ayurvedic practitioners prescribe tailored treatment protocols that encompass a holistic array of therapies, including dietary modifications, herbal remedies, lifestyle adjustments, detoxification practices, and therapeutic interventions such as massage, yoga, and meditation.

Central to Ayurvedic healing is the concept of Dinacharya, or daily routine, which emphasizes the importance of aligning with the natural rhythms of the day to support overall well-being. From rising with the sun and practicing morning rituals of self-care to eating nourishing meals at regular intervals and winding down with calming activities in the evening, Dinacharya offers a framework for harmonizing body, mind, and spirit with the cycles of nature.

In essence, Ayurveda serves as a timeless guide to holistic living, offering not only remedies for alleviating symptoms of illness but also insights into cultivating a life of balance, vitality, and inner harmony. By honoring the unique constitution of each individual and embracing the interconnectedness of body, mind, and spirit, Ayurveda invites us to embark on a journey of self-discovery, self-care, and self-realization, a journey that leads us back to our innate state of wholeness and well-being.

At the heart of Ayurvedic healing lies the profound concept of "Prakriti," which encapsulates an individual's unique constitution and natural state of being. Prakriti encompasses not only physical attributes but also mental and emotional characteristics, representing the intricate interplay of the three doshas, Vata, Pitta, and Kapha, within each person. Understanding one's prakriti is essential in Ayurveda as it serves as the foundation for personalized health and wellness strategies.

Through careful observation and assessment, Ayurvedic practitioners identify the dominant doshas and their relative balance within an individual's prakriti. This knowledge allows for targeted interventions to restore harmony and equilibrium, thereby promoting optimal health and vitality. For example, an individual with a predominant Vata constitution may be advised to adopt grounding practices such as regularity in daily routines, warm and nourishing foods, and gentle forms of exercise to counterbalance Vata's inherent qualities of mobility and dryness.

Ayurveda offers a diverse array of therapeutic modalities to support individuals in aligning with their prakriti and achieving holistic well-being. Medicinal herbs play a central role in Ayurvedic healing, with plants like turmeric, holy basil, and ashwagandha prized for their potent medicinal properties. These herbs are carefully selected and prescribed based on their specific actions on the doshas and their ability to restore balance to the body and mind.

In addition to herbal remedies, Ayurveda advocates for cleansing therapies such as Panchakarma, which aim to detoxify and rejuvenate the body through a series of specialized treatments. Panchakarma therapies, including therapeutic oil massages, herbal steam baths, and cleansing enemas, are tailored to each individual's prakriti and imbalances, facilitating the removal of toxins and restoring the body's innate healing capacity.

Furthermore, Ayurveda emphasizes the importance of lifestyle modifications and dietary adjustments to support overall well-being in alignment with one's prakriti. By adopting practices such as mindful eating, regular exercise, adequate rest, and stress management techniques, individuals can cultivate a lifestyle that fosters balance and vitality in accordance with their unique constitution.

In essence, the concept of prakriti underscores the personalized and holistic approach of Ayurvedic healing, empowering individuals to take an active role in their health and well-being. By understanding and honoring their innate constitution, individuals can make informed choices that promote harmony, resilience, and longevity, allowing them to thrive in body, mind, and spirit.

Yoga, often described as the sister science of Ayurveda, offers a profound pathway to holistic well-being, serving as a bridge between the physical, mental, and spiritual dimensions of existence. Rooted in ancient Vedic teachings, Yoga embodies a comprehensive system of practices designed to awaken consciousness, expand awareness, and cultivate harmony within oneself and with the world.

At the heart of Yoga practice lies the integration of physical postures (asanas), breathing techniques (pranayama), and meditation, which work synergistically to align the body, mind, and spirit. Through the dynamic movements of asanas, individuals engage in a mindful exploration of the body, releasing tension, improving flexibility, and enhancing physical strength and endurance. Each posture is performed with awareness and intention, inviting practitioners to connect deeply with their breath and sensations, cultivating a sense of presence and mindfulness in the present moment.

In tandem with asana practice, pranayama techniques harness the power of breath to regulate the flow of prana, or life force energy, within the body. By consciously directing the breath through various breathing exercises, individuals can balance the subtle energies of the body, calm the mind, and cultivate a sense of inner tranquility and vitality. Pranayama practices range from simple deep breathing exercises to more advanced techniques such as alternate nostril breathing and breath retention, each offering unique benefits for physical, mental, and emotional well-being.

Central to the transformative power of Yoga is the practice of meditation, which serves as a gateway to inner exploration and self-discovery. Through meditation, individuals cultivate a state of inner stillness and awareness, transcending the fluctuations of the mind and accessing deeper layers of consciousness. By observing thoughts, emotions, and sensations with detachment and equanimity, practitioners develop greater clarity, insight, and resilience in the face of life's challenges.

Beyond its physical benefits, Yoga offers profound psychological and spiritual benefits, fostering a sense of interconnectedness, compassion, and inner peace. As individuals deepen their practice, they may experience a profound shift in perspective, recognizing the inherent unity and interconnectedness of all beings and experiencing a deep sense of harmony and belonging in the world.

In essence, Yoga serves as a timeless path to self-realization and liberation, guiding individuals on a journey of self-discovery, transformation, and awakening. By integrating the principles and practices of Yoga into their daily lives, individuals can cultivate greater balance, resilience, and inner peace, allowing them to navigate life's challenges with grace, clarity, and presence.

Traditional herbal remedies have been an integral part of India's holistic healthcare system for centuries, harnessing the healing power of nature to promote health and vitality. Rooted in ancient wisdom and passed down through generations, these remedies offer gentle yet effective solutions for a myriad of health concerns, ranging from common ailments to chronic conditions.

One of the cornerstone herbs in traditional Indian medicine is ashwagandha, also known as Indian ginseng.

Revered for its adaptogenic properties, ashwagandha helps the body adapt to stress, support immune function, and promote overall well-being. Whether consumed as a powder, capsule, or herbal tonic, ashwagandha is prized for its ability to enhance resilience and vitality in the face of life's challenges.

Similarly, triphala, a traditional herbal formula comprised of three fruits , amalaki, bibhitaki, and haritaki , is renowned for its rejuvenating and detoxifying effects. Triphala supports digestive health, promotes regularity, and helps to balance the doshas, making it a versatile remedy for a wide range of gastrointestinal issues.

Ginger and cumin are two other commonly used herbs in traditional Indian medicine, valued for their digestive properties and culinary versatility. Ginger, with its warming and soothing qualities, is often used to alleviate nausea, improve digestion, and reduce inflammation. Cumin, on the other hand, aids in digestion, enhances nutrient absorption, and promotes gut health, making it a staple ingredient in many traditional Indian dishes.

Beyond their physical benefits, traditional herbal remedies embody the deep connection between humans and the natural world, reflecting an ancient understanding of the healing potential inherent in plants, roots, and botanical extracts. Passed down through oral tradition and experiential knowledge, this wisdom is a testament to the resilience and resourcefulness of indigenous cultures, who have cultivated a profound relationship with the earth and its bounty.

In the modern era, there has been a resurgence of interest in traditional herbal medicine, fueled by a growing awareness of the limitations and side effects of conventional pharmaceuticals. As scientific research continues to validate the efficacy of traditional herbal remedies, there is a renewed appreciation for their holistic approach to health and wellness, which seeks to address the root cause of illness and promote balance and harmony in the body.

In essence, traditional herbal remedies are not just potions and elixirs; they are embodiments of ancient wisdom, passed down through generations as a sacred legacy of healing and wholeness. By embracing the wisdom of traditional herbal medicine, individuals can tap into the profound healing potential of nature, reconnecting with the earth and reclaiming their innate capacity for health and vitality.

The resurgence of interest in traditional medicine reflects a broader shift in healthcare paradigms, as people seek alternatives to conventional practices and embrace holistic approaches to wellness. In recent years, there has been a growing recognition of the value of Ayurveda, Yoga, and traditional herbal remedies in promoting health and vitality, not only in India but across the globe. This renewed interest is fueled by a desire for natural, sustainable solutions to health concerns, as well as a growing awareness of the limitations and side effects of conventional pharmaceuticals.

One of the driving forces behind the resurgence of traditional medicine is the growing body of scientific research validating the efficacy and safety of these ancient healing practices. Studies have shown that Ayurvedic treatments, such as herbal remedies, dietary modifications, and lifestyle interventions, can effectively alleviate a wide range of health conditions, from chronic pain and inflammation to digestive disorders and mental health issues. Similarly, research on Yoga has demonstrated its therapeutic benefits for stress reduction, pain management, and improving overall quality of life.

In addition to scientific research, the resurgence of traditional medicine is also fueled by a shift in cultural attitudes towards health and wellness. As people become increasingly disillusioned with the impersonal and profit-driven nature of mainstream healthcare, they are turning to traditional healing modalities that offer a more holistic and patient-centered approach. Ayurveda, with its emphasis on individualized care and preventive medicine, resonates with those seeking personalized solutions to their health concerns, while Yoga offers a holistic approach to wellness that addresses the physical, mental, and spiritual dimensions of health.

Furthermore, the globalization of traditional medicine has played a significant role in its resurgence, as practitioners and enthusiasts around the world share knowledge, resources, and best practices. Ayurvedic clinics and Yoga studios are now commonplace in major cities worldwide, offering a range of services and therapies to promote health and well-being. Similarly, traditional herbal remedies are gaining popularity as people seek natural alternatives to synthetic pharmaceuticals, driven by a desire for sustainability, affordability, and cultural authenticity.

As traditional medicine continues to gain traction in both mainstream and alternative healthcare circles, we are witnessing an integration of traditional and modern healthcare systems that offers the promise of a more holistic and patient-centered approach to wellness. This integration recognizes the value of ancient healing practices in promoting health and vitality, while also acknowledging the advancements of modern medicine in diagnosing and treating acute conditions. By embracing the wisdom of traditional medicine and incorporating it into modern healthcare systems, we have the opportunity to create a more inclusive, accessible, and effective approach to health and wellness for all.

As we embark on our journey through the ancient healing traditions of India, we are guided by the wisdom of the ages, passed down through millennia of human experience and insight. These traditions, rooted in the profound understanding of the interconnectedness of body, mind, and spirit, offer us a holistic approach to health and well-being that transcends the limitations of modern medicine.

At the heart of these ancient healing practices lies Ayurveda, often referred to as the "science of life." This holistic system of medicine recognizes the inherent intelligence of the body and its innate ability to heal itself when given the right support. Through personalized lifestyle recommendations, dietary modifications, and herbal remedies, Ayurveda seeks to restore balance and harmony to the body, mind, and spirit, thereby promoting optimal health and vitality.

Complementing the principles of Ayurveda is the practice of Yoga, which serves as a pathway to union between body, mind, and spirit. Through the practice of physical postures (asanas), breathing techniques (pranayama), and meditation, Yoga cultivates self-awareness, inner peace, and spiritual growth. It offers a holistic approach to wellness that addresses the root causes of disease and promotes balance and harmony in all aspects of life.

In addition to Ayurveda and Yoga, traditional herbal medicine plays a vital role in India's holistic healthcare system, harnessing the healing power of nature to promote health and vitality. From the rejuvenating effects of ashwagandha to the digestive benefits of ginger and cumin, these natural remedies offer gentle yet effective solutions for a wide range of health concerns.

As we delve deeper into the ancient healing traditions of India, we are reminded of the profound connection between humanity and the natural world. These traditions teach us to honor the rhythms of nature, to respect the wisdom of the earth, and to live in harmony with the cycles of life. They remind us that health is not merely the absence of disease but a state of vibrant balance and well-being in which body, mind, and spirit are in alignment.

Furthermore, the resurgence of interest in traditional medicine reflects a growing recognition of the limitations and side effects of conventional pharmaceuticals. As people seek natural, sustainable solutions to their health concerns, they are turning to ancient healing modalities that offer a more holistic and patient-centered approach to wellness.

Moreover, the integration of traditional and modern healthcare systems offers the promise of a more inclusive, accessible, and effective approach to health and wellness for all. By embracing the wisdom of traditional medicine and incorporating it into mainstream healthcare practices, we have the opportunity to create a healthcare system that is truly holistic, addressing the physical, emotional, and spiritual needs of individuals.

In conclusion, as we journey through the ancient healing traditions of India, let us embrace the wisdom of the past and the promise of the future. May we honor the timeless teachings of Ayurveda, Yoga, and traditional herbal medicine as we embark on a journey of self-discovery, healing, and transformation. Together, let us strive to achieve optimal health and well-being in body, mind, and spirit, honoring the interconnectedness of all life and the sacredness of the healing journey.

CHAPTER X

The Tribal Cultures of India

Madhya Pradesh, often called the "Heart of India" due to its central location, is a state rich in cultural diversity, particularly known for its numerous tribal communities. The state's landscape is dotted with forests, rivers, and ancient monuments, creating a backdrop where tribal cultures thrive. The tribes of Madhya Pradesh include the Gonds, Bhils, Baigas, Sahariyas, and Korkus, each with distinct languages, traditions, and lifestyles. These tribes have preserved their unique cultural identities through their customs, rituals, and artistic expressions.

The Gonds, the largest tribal group in Madhya Pradesh, are known for their vibrant art, music, and dance. Gond art, characterized by intricate patterns and vibrant colours, often depicts their myths, gods, and daily life. This art form is not merely decorative but also deeply symbolic, representing the tribe's connection to nature and their spiritual beliefs. The Gonds also celebrate numerous festivals, with dances like Karma and Saila being integral to their cultural expression. These dances, performed during various festivals and community gatherings, are accompanied by traditional musical instruments such as the dhol, mandal, and flute, creating a lively and rhythmic atmosphere.

The Baiga tribe, renowned for their deep knowledge of forest herbs and traditional medicine, are considered the healers of the forest. Their practices are rooted in a profound understanding of the natural world and its healing properties. The Baigas have a unique spiritual worldview, where every element of nature is imbued with spiritual significance. Their dances, performed during festivals and rituals, are not just a form of entertainment but a medium to connect with the divine and seek blessings for health and prosperity. The Baiga dance, characterized by rhythmic movements and elaborate costumes, reflects their connection to nature and their spiritual beliefs.

The Bhils, known for their archery skills, have a rich cultural heritage that includes a vibrant tradition of folk art and music. Bhil paintings, particularly the Pithora paintings, are renowned for their vibrant colours and intricate designs. These paintings, often depicting scenes from daily life, mythology, and nature, are created on the walls of their homes as a form of worship and to bring good fortune. Bhil festivals, such as Bhagoria, are lively and colourful events that highlight the tribe's cultural richness. During Bhagoria, young men and women dress in their finest clothes and participate in dance and music, celebrating the harvest season with great enthusiasm.

The Sahariya tribe, primarily found in the forests of Madhya Pradesh, leads a traditional way of life that is closely tied to their natural surroundings. Their dances, like Lur and Swang, performed during weddings and festivals, are a vibrant expression of their cultural heritage. These dances are accompanied by traditional music and are performed in a circle, symbolizing community unity and harmony. The Sahariyas are also known for their craftsmanship, particularly in basket weaving and pottery, which are integral to their daily life and economy.

Madhya Pradesh's tribal communities are also known for their exceptional craftsmanship. The traditional crafts of these tribes, such as weaving intricate textiles, beadwork, and pottery, are not only a source of income but also a means of preserving their cultural heritage. Their crafts' unique designs and motifs are often inspired by their surroundings and hold significant cultural meanings. These crafts are passed down through generations, ensuring the continuity of their traditional skills and artistry.

Tribal festivals in Madhya Pradesh are a time of vibrant celebration, marked by music, dance, and rituals that reinforce community bonds and cultural identity. Festivals such as the Karma festival, celebrated by the Gonds, involve dancing around a tree symbolizing fertility and prosperity. These festivals provide an opportunity for the tribes to come together, share their traditions, and pass them down to the younger generations. The tribal way of life in Madhya Pradesh is deeply intertwined with nature. Their traditional knowledge of agriculture, forest conservation, and herbal medicine has been passed down through generations. This harmonious relationship with nature is reflected in their cultural practices, rituals, and daily life, emphasizing sustainability and respect for the environment.

Despite the challenges posed by modernization and external influences, the tribal communities of Madhya Pradesh continue to strive for the preservation and promotion of their cultural heritage. Efforts by the government and various organizations to support tribal arts, crafts, and education are helping to ensure that these rich traditions are not lost. Madhya Pradesh, with its diverse and vibrant tribal cultures, offers a unique glimpse into a way of life that is deeply rooted in tradition and nature. The cultural heritage of its tribal communities is a testament to the resilience and creativity of these indigenous people, who continue to celebrate and preserve their identity in the heart of India.

The Gonds, the largest tribal group in Madhya Pradesh, is a community with a rich cultural heritage that encompasses vibrant art, music, and dance. Their artistic expression is not just a form of aesthetic enjoyment but is deeply intertwined with their social and spiritual life.

Gond art is renowned for its intricate patterns and vibrant colours, which are often used to depict a wide range of subjects, from mythological tales and gods to scenes of daily life and nature. This art form, traditionally created on the walls of their homes, has now found a place on canvases, allowing a broader audience to appreciate its beauty. The themes of Gond art are deeply rooted in the natural environment and the folklore of the Gond people. Common motifs include animals, birds, trees, and other elements of the natural world, often rendered in a stylized and symbolic manner. The use of dots and lines to create complex patterns is a distinctive feature of this art, reflecting the detailed and meticulous nature of the work.

The stories depicted in Gond paintings often have moral or spiritual messages, with a strong emphasis on the interconnectedness of life. This connection to nature is not only a reflection of the Gond people's reverence for the environment but also a representation of their belief in the presence of spiritual forces in all aspects of the natural world.

Music and dance are integral to Gond culture, serving as a means of storytelling, celebration, and spiritual expression. Folk dances like Karma and Saila are central to their cultural festivities. The Karma dance, performed during the Karma festival, is particularly significant. It involves rhythmic movements and is performed around a tree or branch, symbolizing fertility and prosperity. The dancers form a circle and move in synchronized steps, often accompanied by songs that tell stories of love, courage, and the deities. The dance is both a communal activity and a spiritual one, fostering a sense of unity and continuity among the participants.

The Saila dance, typically performed during the post-harvest season, is another vibrant expression of Gond culture. This dance involves intricate footwork and is performed by young men who form a circle or a line. The Saila dance is not only a celebration of the harvest but also a way to express gratitude to the gods for a bountiful crop. The energetic movements and the rhythmic beats create an atmosphere of joy and festivity, reflecting the community's close ties to agriculture and the cycles of nature.

Traditional musical instruments play a crucial role in these dances, providing rhythm and enhancing the overall experience. The dhol, a double-headed drum, is one of the primary instruments used, producing deep and resonant sounds that drive the dance's rhythm. The mandal, a type of tambourine, adds a higher-pitched, melodic accompaniment, creating a rich and layered musical texture. These instruments often handcrafted from natural materials, are not only tools for music but also cultural artifacts that carry the legacy of the Gond people's craftsmanship and traditions.

The dances are often accompanied by folk songs that are passed down through generations. These songs, sung in the Gondi language, often tell stories of ancestral heroes, gods, and the natural world. They are a repository of the community's history, values, and beliefs, ensuring that their cultural heritage is preserved and transmitted to future generations.

The performance of these dances during festivals and celebrations is a testament to the resilience and vibrancy of

Gond culture. These events are not just entertainment but are deeply embedded in the social and spiritual fabric of the community. They provide an opportunity for the Gond people to come together, reaffirm their cultural identity, and celebrate their shared heritage. In a world that is increasingly influenced by modernization and globalization, these traditional practices serve as a vital link to the past, fostering a sense of continuity and belonging.

Overall, the Gonds' art, music, and dance are vital components of their cultural identity, reflecting their deep connection to nature, their rich mythological traditions, and their communal values. Through their vibrant and expressive cultural practices, the Gonds continue to preserve and celebrate their unique heritage.

The Baiga tribe, known for their deep knowledge of forest herbs and traditional medicine, are considered the healers of the forest. Their expertise in herbal medicine is a cornerstone of their identity, with an extensive understanding of the medicinal properties of various plants, roots, and herbs found in their natural surroundings. This knowledge has been passed down through generations, enabling the Baiga to treat a wide range of ailments using natural remedies. Their reputation as healers extends beyond their community, with people from neighboring areas often seeking their expertise.

The Baiga's spiritual practices and rituals are deeply connected to nature, reflecting their belief in the symbiotic relationship between humans and the natural world. They worship a variety of deities, each associated with different aspects of nature, such as forests, rivers, and mountains. These deities are believed to inhabit specific natural sites, which are considered sacred. The Baiga perform rituals to honor these deities, seeking their blessings for health, prosperity, and protection. These rituals are elaborate and involve offerings of food, flowers, and other natural items, as well as the chanting of prayers and the performance of dances.

The Baiga dance is a significant aspect of their culture, showcasing their connection to the natural world and their spiritual beliefs. This dance is performed during various festivals and rituals, marking important events in the community's life, such as the harvest season, religious ceremonies, and life cycle events like births and marriages. The dance is characterized by its rhythmic movements and vibrant energy, reflecting the joy and vitality of the Baiga people.

The Baiga dance is not just a form of entertainment but also a spiritual practice. It is believed to invoke the presence of the deities and spirits, creating a sacred space where the community can connect with the divine. The dancers, often adorned in traditional attire made from natural materials, move in sync with the beats of drums and other musical instruments. The traditional costumes are typically made from locally sourced materials like cotton and adorned with colourful patterns and beads, symbolizing their cultural heritage.

The music accompanying the Baiga dance is an essential component of the performance, enhancing the overall experience and creating a sense of unity among the participants. Traditional instruments such as the mandal (a type of tambourine), the dhol (a double-headed drum), and the flute are commonly used. The rhythmic beats of these instruments guide the dancers' movements, while the melodies played on the flute add a lyrical quality to the performance.

Songs sung during the dance often tell stories of the tribe's history, mythology, and daily life, serving as a means of preserving and transmitting cultural knowledge. These songs are rich in metaphor and imagery, reflecting the Baiga's deep connection to nature and their spiritual worldview. The lyrics often celebrate the beauty of the forest, the bounty of the harvest, and the strength and resilience of the community.

In addition to their role in rituals and celebrations, the Baiga dance and music also serve as a means of social cohesion. These performances bring the community together, reinforcing bonds of kinship and shared identity. They provide an opportunity for the Baiga to express their collective emotions, whether it be joy, sorrow, or reverence. Through these cultural practices, the Baiga maintain a strong sense of community and continuity, even in the face of external pressures and changes.

The Baiga's way of life, deeply intertwined with the forest and its resources, underscores their commitment to sustainable living and environmental stewardship. Their knowledge of the forest and its biodiversity is not only a source of livelihood but also a testament to their adaptive strategies and resilience. By preserving their traditional practices and passing them down to younger generations, the Baiga ensure that their cultural heritage and ecological wisdom continue to thrive.

In conclusion, the Baiga tribe's profound knowledge of forest herbs and traditional medicine, coupled with their spiritual practices and vibrant dance traditions, highlight their deep connection to nature and their rich cultural heritage. Their holistic way of life, which integrates ecological wisdom, spiritual beliefs, and artistic expression, offers valuable insights into the sustainable relationship between humans and the natural world. Through their enduring traditions, the Baiga continue to celebrate and preserve their unique identity as the healers of the forest.

The Bhils, known for their archery skills, are one of the largest tribal communities in India, with a rich cultural heritage that reflects their deep connection to their land and traditions. The Bhil community is spread across several states, including Madhya Pradesh, Gujarat, Rajasthan, and Maharashtra, each region contributing to the diversity of Bhil culture. Despite regional variations, certain elements, such as their expertise in archery, vibrant art, and lively festivals, remain central to their identity.

Archery, an ancient skill of the Bhils, is not just a means of hunting but also a symbol of their martial heritage and self-reliance. Historically, the Bhils were renowned for their archery skills, which they used for hunting, defense, and even as a sport. Archery competitions and displays of skill are still a part of Bhil cultural events, reflecting the community's pride in this traditional expertise.

One of the most distinctive aspects of Bhil culture is their folk art, particularly the Pithora paintings. These paintings are more than mere decorative art; they are a form of storytelling and worship. Created primarily by the Bhilala sub-group of the Bhils, Pithora paintings are traditionally made on the walls of homes and community spaces to mark auspicious occasions, seek divine blessings, or celebrate significant events. The process of creating a Pithora painting is a ritual in itself, often involving the entire community. The vibrant and intricate designs depict various deities, animals, and scenes from daily life, reflecting the Bhils' close relationship with nature and their spiritual beliefs.

The themes of Pithora paintings often revolve around the gods and goddesses worshipped by the Bhils, such as Baba Pithora, the main deity, who is believed to bring prosperity and protect the community. These paintings also depict scenes of agriculture, hunting, and celebrations, capturing the essence of Bhil life and traditions. The use of bold colours and dynamic compositions in Pithora paintings creates a sense of movement and vitality, mirroring the energetic spirit of the Bhil people.

Bhagoria, one of the most prominent festivals of the Bhils, is a colourful and lively harvest festival that highlights their vibrant traditions and strong sense of community. Celebrated primarily in the regions of Madhya Pradesh and Maharashtra, Bhagoria marks the end of the agricultural season and the onset of spring. The festival's name is derived from 'bhagor', meaning 'to run away', referring to an old custom where young couples would elope during the festival.

Bhagoria is celebrated with great enthusiasm and involves a series of fairs held in various villages over several days. These fairs are a riot of colours, sounds, and activities, with people dressing in their finest traditional attire, adorned with jewelry and intricate tattoos. The fairs feature a variety of stalls selling local handicrafts, food, and agricultural produce, along with music and dance performances that showcase the rich cultural heritage of the Bhils.

One of the most anticipated aspects of Bhagoria is the traditional dance and music. Bhil dances are characterized by their energetic movements and rhythmic beats, often accompanied by traditional musical instruments like the dhol, mandal, and flute. The dancers, both men and women, move in synchronized patterns, creating a vibrant spectacle that captivates the audience. The songs sung during these dances are typically folk songs that tell stories of love, heroism, and daily life, passed down through generations.

The social aspect of Bhagoria is equally important. The festival serves as a meeting place for young people to find potential life partners, continuing the tradition of courtship and marriage that has been a part of Bhil culture for centuries. This aspect of the festival, where young couples publicly express their interest in each other, is celebrated with much cheer and acceptance by the community, reflecting the Bhils' progressive and open-minded social values.

In addition to Bhagoria, the Bhils celebrate a range of other festivals that highlight their cultural diversity and communal spirit. Festivals such as Diwali, Holi, and Dussehra are celebrated with unique Bhil customs and rituals, adding to the richness of their cultural tapestry. Each festival is an opportunity for the Bhils to come together, reaffirm their cultural identity, and strengthen their community bonds.

The Bhils' rich cultural heritage, encompassing their skills in archery, vibrant folk art, and lively festivals, offers a fascinating glimpse into their way of life. Through their traditions, the Bhils maintain a strong connection to their history, their land, and each other, ensuring that their unique cultural identity continues to thrive in the modern world.

The Sahariya tribe, primarily found in the forests of Madhya Pradesh, is a community known for its close-knit communities and traditional way of life. Living in harmony with their natural surroundings, the Sahariyas have developed unique cultural practices that reflect their deep connection to the land and each other.

One of the most distinctive aspects of Sahariya culture is their traditional dances, such as the Lur and Swang. These dances are not only forms of entertainment but also significant expressions of their cultural heritage and communal harmony. They are typically performed during weddings, festivals, and other celebratory occasions, serving as a means of social cohesion and community bonding.

The Lur dance, characterized by its rhythmic movements and energetic footwork, is often performed by both men and women in a circular formation. The dancers move in sync with the beats of traditional musical instruments like drums and flutes, creating a lively and vibrant atmosphere. The dance is accompanied by songs sung in the Sahariya language, which often narrate stories of their history, mythology, and daily life. The lyrics of these songs are rich in metaphor and symbolism, reflecting the Sahariyas' deep spiritual connection to nature and their surroundings.

Similarly, the Swang dance is another integral part of Sahariya culture, often performed during agricultural festivals and religious ceremonies. This dance is characterized by its graceful movements and intricate choreography, with dancers often wearing colourful costumes adorned with traditional jewelry and accessories. The Swang dance is a celebration of life, fertility, and abundance, reflecting the Sahariyas' reliance on the land for their livelihood and sustenance.

The performance of these traditional dances is a communal affair, with the entire community coming together to celebrate important milestones and events. It is not uncommon for multiple generations to participate in the dances, with elders passing down their knowledge and skills to younger members of the tribe. These dances serve as a means of cultural transmission, ensuring that the traditions and values of the Sahariya tribe are preserved and passed on to future generations.

In addition to their role in cultural preservation, the Sahariya dances also play a crucial role in fostering social cohesion and communal harmony within the tribe. They provide an opportunity for members of the community to come together, forge bonds of friendship and solidarity, and celebrate their shared identity. The dances serve as a unifying force, transcending differences of age, gender, and social status, and reinforcing the sense of belonging and interconnectedness among the Sahariyas.

Overall, the Sahariya dances, such as the Lur and Swang, are not just forms of artistic expression but also powerful symbols of cultural identity and communal harmony. They embody the spirit of the Sahariya tribe, reflecting their values, beliefs, and way of life. Through these dances, the Sahariyas continue to celebrate their rich cultural heritage and maintain their strong sense of community in the face of modernization and social change.

Madhya Pradesh's tribal communities are renowned for their exceptional craftsmanship, which encompasses a wide range of traditional arts and crafts. These crafts, including weaving intricate textiles, beadwork, and pottery, are not only sources of income for the tribes but also vital means of preserving their cultural heritage and identity.

Textile weaving is one of the oldest and most practiced crafts among Madhya Pradesh's tribal communities. Each tribe has its unique weaving techniques, patterns, and designs, passed down through generations. The fabrics produced by these tribes are often characterized by vibrant colours, intricate motifs, and skilled craftsmanship. For example, the Gond tribe is known for its use of geometric patterns and natural dyes in their textiles, while the Bhils are renowned for their skillful use of tie-dye and block-printing techniques. These textiles are not only functional but also carry deep cultural significance, often used in traditional attire, rituals, and ceremonies.

Beadwork is another prominent craft among Madhya Pradesh's tribal communities, with intricate beadwork adorning clothing, jewelry, and decorative items. The beads used in these crafts are often sourced from natural materials such as seeds, shells, and stones, and are meticulously arranged to create elaborate designs and patterns. Beadwork holds significant cultural and symbolic meanings for the tribes, often used to convey messages of status, identity, and spirituality. For example, certain beadwork patterns may signify belonging to a specific tribe or clan, while others may represent auspicious symbols or protective talismans.

Pottery is also an integral part of Madhya Pradesh's tribal crafts, with each tribe having its unique pottery-making traditions and styles. From utilitarian pots and vessels to decorative figurines and ceremonial objects, pottery plays a diverse range of roles in tribal life. The Sahariya tribe, for example, is known for its terracotta pottery, often decorated with intricate carvings and designs inspired by nature. Pottery-making techniques are typically passed down from one generation to the next, with knowledge and skills transmitted orally and through hands-on practice.

The designs and motifs found in Madhya Pradesh's tribal crafts are often inspired by the tribes' surroundings, reflecting their close relationship with nature and the environment. For example, patterns may depict animals, plants, landscapes, or celestial bodies, each carrying symbolic meanings and cultural significance. These motifs not only beautify the crafts but also serve as visual narratives, preserving traditional stories, myths, and beliefs for future generations.

In addition to preserving cultural heritage, tribal crafts also serve as a means of economic empowerment for the communities. Many tribal artisans rely on their craft skills as a primary source of income, selling their products in local markets, fairs, and exhibitions, as well as to tourists and collectors. Organizations and initiatives supporting tribal crafts, such as cooperatives and NGOs, provide training, marketing assistance, and fair trade opportunities, enabling artisans to sustain their livelihoods while preserving their cultural traditions.

Overall, Madhya Pradesh's tribal crafts are not just objects of beauty but also repositories of cultural knowledge, history, and identity. They reflect the tribes' creativity, ingenuity, and resilience, as well as their deep connection to the land and their heritage. By continuing to practice and celebrate their traditional crafts, Madhya Pradesh's tribal communities ensure that their rich cultural legacy lives on for future generations to appreciate and cherish.

Tribal festivals in Madhya Pradesh are a time of vibrant celebration, marked by music, dance, and rituals that reinforce community bonds and cultural identity. Festivals such as the Karma festival, celebrated by the Gonds, involve dancing around a tree symbolizing fertility and prosperity. These festivals provide an opportunity for the tribes to come together, share their traditions, and pass them down to the younger generations.

The tribal way of life in Madhya Pradesh is deeply intertwined with nature. Their traditional knowledge of agriculture, forest conservation, and herbal medicine has been passed down through generations. This harmonious relationship with nature is reflected in their cultural practices, rituals, and daily life, emphasizing sustainability and respect for the environment.

Despite the challenges posed by modernization and external influences, the tribal communities of Madhya Pradesh continue to strive for the preservation and promotion of their cultural heritage. Efforts by the government and various organizations to support tribal arts, crafts, and education are helping to ensure that these rich traditions are not lost.

Madhya Pradesh, with its diverse and vibrant tribal cultures, offers a unique glimpse into a way of life that is deeply rooted in tradition and nature. The cultural heritage of its tribal communities is a testament to the resilience and creativity of these indigenous people, who continue to celebrate and preserve their identity in the heart of India.

Odisha, with its diverse topography ranging from coastal plains to hilly terrains, hosts a rich tapestry of tribal cultures. These indigenous communities, deeply connected to their land and traditions, play a significant role in the state's cultural mosaic.

One of the prominent tribal communities in Odisha is the Kondh tribe. They are renowned for their agricultural practices, especially terrace farming on the slopes of the Eastern Ghats. The Kondhs' traditional knowledge of sustainable farming methods, passed down through generations, highlights their harmonious relationship with the land. Moreover, their festivals, like the Kondh Kui festival, are vibrant celebrations that showcase their cultural vibrancy, with rituals, music, and dances reflecting their spiritual beliefs and social cohesion.

Another notable tribe is the Santal tribe, predominantly found in the Mayurbhanj district. The Santals are known for their craftsmanship, particularly in woodwork and pottery. Their intricate wood carvings depict scenes from nature, mythology, and daily life, serving as a visual narrative of their cultural heritage. Additionally, Santal music and dance are integral parts of their social and religious ceremonies, fostering community bonding and preserving ancestral traditions.

In the hilly terrains of Koraput district, the Bonda tribe thrives with its distinct cultural identity. The Bondas' traditional attire, adorned with colourful beads and brass ornaments, reflects their aesthetic sensibility and craftsmanship. Furthermore, their egalitarian social structure, governed by village councils, underscores their sense of community and democratic values. Festivals like Maghe Parab provide opportunities for the Bondas to celebrate their cultural heritage through traditional dances, songs, and rituals.

The Dongria Kondh tribe, inhabiting the Niyamgiri hills, epitomizes the symbiotic relationship between tribal communities and their natural environment. They worship Niyam Raja, the deity of the Niyamgiri hills, and consider the forests sacred. Dongria Kondhs' traditional knowledge of herbal medicine and biodiversity conservation underscores their ecological wisdom and sustainable lifestyle. Their festivals, such as Niyamraja Parab, serve as occasions for spiritual rejuvenation and reaffirmation of their cultural identity.

In essence, Odisha's tribal communities embody the state's rich cultural heritage and environmental stewardship. Their customs, languages, and way of life are testaments to their resilience and adaptability in the face of modernization. By preserving their age-old traditions and harmonious relationship with nature, these tribes continue to enrich Odisha's cultural landscape and inspire future generations.

The Kondh tribe, renowned for its vibrant cultural heritage, occupies a significant place among Odisha's diverse tribal communities. Rooted in agriculture and spirituality, the Kondhs' way of life is deeply intertwined with their natural surroundings, shaping their rituals, festivals, and everyday practices.

At the heart of Kondh culture are their festivals, which serve as vibrant expressions of their cultural identity and communal bonding. The Kondh Kui festival, in particular, stands out as a celebration of the harvest season and a time for giving thanks to the land and the deities. During this festival, the Kondhs come together to perform colourful rituals, accompanied by lively music and energetic dances. These rituals often involve offerings of rice, fruits, and other agricultural produce to the gods, symbolizing gratitude for the bounties of nature.

The traditional attire of the Kondh people is another striking aspect of their cultural heritage. Adorned with intricate patterns and vibrant colours, their clothing reflects not only their aesthetic sensibilities but also their deep reverence for nature. The motifs used in their attire often depict elements from the natural world, such as flowers, leaves, and animals, symbolizing the Kondhs' close connection to their environment. Additionally, the use of natural dyes derived from plants and minerals adds to the authenticity and eco-friendliness of their traditional clothing.

Spirituality plays a central role in Kondh culture, with a belief system deeply rooted in animism and ancestor worship. The Kondhs venerate various deities associated with nature, fertility, and agriculture, seeking their blessings for a bountiful harvest and prosperity. Rituals and ceremonies conducted by the Kondh priests, known as 'pans,' often involve offerings, prayers, and sacred chants performed to appease the spirits and maintain harmony with the natural world.

Furthermore, music and dance form integral parts of Kondh ceremonies and festivities, serving as expressions of joy, unity, and cultural pride. Traditional musical instruments like drums, flutes, and stringed instruments accompany the rhythmic movements of Kondh dancers, creating an immersive and celebratory atmosphere. These dances passed down through generations, are not only sources of entertainment but also vehicles for transmitting cultural knowledge and values to younger members of the community.

In essence, the Kondh tribe's rich cultural heritage, deeply rooted in agriculture, spirituality, and community, is a testament to their resilience and adaptability in the face of social and environmental changes. Through their festivals, rituals, attire, and artistic expressions, the Kondhs continue to preserve and celebrate their unique identity, ensuring that their cultural legacy thrives for generations to come.

The Santal tribe, predominantly residing in the Mayurbhanj district of Odisha, is celebrated for its vibrant cultural heritage, which encompasses rich oral traditions, lively music, and exquisite craftsmanship. Rooted in their deep connection to nature and community bonds, Santal culture thrives through various artistic expressions and communal celebrations.

Central to Santal culture are their rich oral traditions, where storytelling plays a pivotal role in passing down ancestral knowledge, myths, and folklore from one generation to the next. Elders within the community serve as custodians of these narratives, weaving intricate tales that reflect the Santals' worldview, beliefs, and values. Through storytelling sessions held during gatherings and festivals, Santal families and communities uphold their cultural heritage and strengthen social ties.

Music is another cornerstone of Santal culture, with traditional instruments like the banam (a stringed instrument) and madol (a drum) adding rhythmic accompaniment to their spirited dances and festivities. Santal music is characterized by its melodious tunes and vibrant beats, evoking a sense of joy and celebration. During festivals such as Sohrai and Mage Parab, the rhythmic sounds of these instruments fill the air as Santal communities come together to rejoice and honor their cultural traditions.

Santal festivals hold a special place in community life, serving as occasions for joyous celebrations and collective bonding. Sohrai, celebrated during the harvest season, and Mage Parab, marking the onset of the spring season, are among the most significant festivals observed by the Santal tribe. During these festivals, families gather to share stories of their ancestors, sing traditional songs, and indulge in sumptuous feasts prepared with seasonal ingredients. These festive occasions not only reinforce cultural identity but also foster a sense of unity and solidarity among Santal communities.

In addition to their rich oral traditions and vibrant music, the Santal tribe is renowned for its intricate woodcraft, which reflects their artistic prowess and reverence for nature. Santal craftsmen skillfully carve intricate designs and motifs into wood, creating a wide range of artifacts, including decorative items, household utensils, and musical instruments. These woodcrafts not only serve utilitarian purposes but also carry cultural significance, symbolizing the Santals' craftsmanship and connection to their natural surroundings.

Overall, the Santal tribe's rich cultural heritage, characterized by its rich oral traditions, vibrant music, and exquisite craftsmanship, is a testament to their resilience, creativity, and communal spirit. Through their artistic expressions and festive celebrations, the Santals continue to uphold their cultural legacy and forge strong bonds of kinship and belonging within their communities.

Nestled in the hilly terrains of Koraput district, the Bonda tribe is known for its distinctive culture, characterized by elaborate ornaments, traditional attire, and unique social structures. The Bondas' traditional dances, performed during festivals like Maghe Parab and Chaiti Parab, are a vibrant display of their cultural heritage and communal harmony. Their close-knit communities and strong sense of identity are reflected in their rituals, customs, and everyday life.

Inhabiting the Niyamgiri hills of Rayagada and Kalahandi districts, the Dongria Kondh tribe is renowned for its deep connection to their ancestral lands and natural surroundings. Their festivals, such as the Niyamraja Parab, are occasions for spiritual renewal and communal bonding, where rituals, prayers, and cultural performances play a central role. The Dongria Kondhs' traditional knowledge of agriculture, herbal medicine, and sustainable living reflects their harmonious relationship with the environment and their commitment to preserving their cultural heritage.

Certainly! Let's explore further:

The North-East region of India is home to a plethora of indigenous tribal communities, each with its unique customs, languages, and traditions. These tribes have thrived amidst the region's breathtaking landscapes, including lush hills, verdant valleys, and dense forests, which have shaped their way of life and cultural practices over centuries.

Nagaland, with its diverse Naga tribes such as the Angami, Ao, Lotha, and Sumi, is renowned for its rich oral traditions, vibrant festivals, and intricate craftsmanship. Festivals like the Hornbill Festival serve as grand showcases of Naga culture, featuring traditional dances, music, and handicrafts, while also providing opportunities for cultural exchange and solidarity among tribes.

Manipur boasts a vibrant cultural landscape, with indigenous tribes like the Naga, Kuki, and Manipuri Meitei contributing to its rich tapestry of traditions. Manipuri Meitei's classical dance forms, such as Manipuri Ras Leela, are celebrated for their grace and beauty, while festivals like Chavang Kut among the Kuki tribes are marked by traditional dances, songs, and rituals, reflecting their agricultural heritage and community bonds.

Mizoram is known for its Mizo tribes, who are renowned for their colourful festivals, vibrant music, and intricate bamboo craftsmanship. Festivals like Chapchar Kut and Mim Kut are occasions for joyous celebrations, where traditional dances, songs, and feasting bring communities together, reinforcing cultural identity and social cohesion.

In Meghalaya, the Khasi, Garo, and Jaintia tribes coexist harmoniously, celebrating festivals like Shad Suk Mynsiem and Behdeinkhlam with traditional dances, songs, and rituals that reflect their reverence for nature and community bonds. The lush landscapes of Meghalaya also inspire traditional crafts like handwoven textiles and intricate bamboo work, which are integral to the cultural identity of the indigenous tribes.

Arunachal Pradesh is home to a diverse array of indigenous tribes, including the Nyishi, Adi, Apatani, and Monpa, each with its unique customs and traditions. Festivals like Losar, Reh, and Si-Donyi are celebrated with traditional dances, prayers, and rituals, symbolizing the cultural heritage and spiritual beliefs of the tribes, while traditional crafts like handwoven textiles and bamboo work reflect their artistic prowess and cultural diversity.

Tripura's indigenous tribes, including the Tripuri and Jamatia, celebrate festivals like Kharchi Puja and Garia Puja with great fervor, showcasing their cultural vibrancy and religious fervor through traditional dances, songs, and rituals. Handloom textiles, bamboo and cane products, and pottery are integral to Tripura's traditional crafts, highlighting the artistic skills and cultural heritage of the indigenous tribes.

Assam's diverse tribal communities, including the Bodo, Karbi, and Mishing, celebrate festivals like Bwisagu and Baishagu with traditional dances, songs, and rituals, symbolizing their cultural resilience and unity. Handloom textiles, bamboo and cane products, and pottery are also prominent in Assam's traditional crafts, reflecting the artistic expression and cultural identity of the indigenous tribes.

The North-East region of India is a melting pot of diverse tribal cultures, each with its unique customs, languages, and traditions. Despite the challenges of modernization and globalization, these indigenous tribes continue to uphold their rich cultural heritage, fostering a sense of pride and identity among their members and contributing to the vibrant cultural tapestry of India's North-East.

The Naga tribes, comprising diverse ethnic groups such as the Angami, Ao, Lotha, and others, have a rich cultural heritage deeply rooted in their warrior traditions, vibrant festivals, and oral traditions. Nestled in the verdant hills of Nagaland, these tribes have cultivated a strong sense of identity and community, which is evident in their rituals, ceremonies, and everyday life.

Warrior traditions have been a significant aspect of Naga culture, with a history of headhunting and inter-tribal warfare that has shaped their social structure and values. While these practices have largely faded away with modernization and Christianity, elements of the Naga warrior ethos still resonate in their festivals and ceremonies, symbolizing courage, valor, and resilience.

The Hornbill Festival stands as a spectacular showcase of Naga culture, drawing visitors from across the globe to witness the vibrancy and diversity of Naga tribes. Held annually in Nagaland's Kisama village, the festival features traditional dances, music performances, indigenous games, and crafts exhibitions, providing a platform for Naga communities to celebrate their cultural heritage and showcase their artistic talents.

Central to Naga culture is their reverence for nature, with a deep spiritual connection to the land, forests, and rivers that sustain their livelihoods. Traditional Naga beliefs are often animistic, attributing spiritual significance to natural phenomena and elements of the environment. Rituals and ceremonies conducted by Naga shamans or village elders are aimed at appeasing ancestral spirits and nature deities, seeking their blessings for bountiful harvests, fertility, and prosperity.

Community cohesion and solidarity are integral to Naga society, with strong bonds forged through shared history, traditions, and experiences. Village councils, comprising respected elders and leaders, play a crucial role in decision-making and conflict resolution, ensuring harmony and consensus within the community. Festivals, weddings, and other social gatherings serve as occasions for strengthening these communal ties, with rituals, feasting, and storytelling fostering a sense of belonging and mutual support among Naga tribes.

In everyday life, Naga traditions and customs permeate various aspects of social interaction, family life, and religious practices. Traditional attire, adorned with intricate patterns and symbolic motifs, reflects cultural identity and status within the community. Folk songs, myths, and legends passed down through generations preserve Naga history and wisdom, enriching the fabric of their oral traditions.

The Naga tribes of Nagaland embody a vibrant cultural tapestry woven from warrior traditions, festive celebrations, reverence for nature, and strong community bonds. Despite the challenges of modernization and cultural change, Naga culture continues to thrive, evolving and adapting while retaining its essence and unique identity.

The Khasi tribe, nestled in the lush landscapes of Meghalaya, stands out for its unique matrilineal society, vibrant festivals, and deep reverence for nature. Their cultural practices, rooted in centuries-old traditions, reflect a harmonious relationship between the community, the environment, and their rich cultural heritage.

One of the distinctive features of Khasi society is its matrilineal system, where descent, inheritance, and familial lineage are traced through the female line. This matriarchal structure shapes social norms, family dynamics, and gender roles within Khasi communities, fostering a sense of empowerment and equality among women. It is not uncommon to find women taking on leadership roles, managing household affairs, and playing active roles in decision-making processes.

Khasi festivals, such as Shad Suk Mynsiem and Behdeinkhlam, are vibrant celebrations that highlight the tribe's cultural richness and spiritual beliefs. Shad Suk Mynsiem, also known as the 'Dance of the Joyful Heart,' is a harvest festival celebrated with great enthusiasm, featuring traditional dances, music performances, and rituals that express gratitude to the deities for a bountiful harvest. Behdeinkhlam, on the other hand, is a festival that celebrates the triumph of good over evil, with rituals like the symbolic 'Rath (chariot) Race' and 'Tug of War' representing the collective effort to ward off malevolent spirits and bring prosperity to the community.

The Khasis' reverence for their ancestral lands is deeply ingrained in their cultural practices and spiritual beliefs. Sacred groves, known as 'law kyntangs,' are protected forest areas regarded as abodes of deities and ancestral spirits. These groves serve as biodiversity hotspots and play a crucial role in conserving the region's flora and fauna. Traditional farming practices, such as jhum cultivation (slash-and-burn agriculture), are conducted in harmony with nature, with rituals and ceremonies performed to seek blessings for a fruitful harvest and environmental sustainability.

Moreover, Khasi folklore, oral traditions, and rituals are imbued with reverence for nature, with myths and legends often portraying the natural world as inhabited by spirits and supernatural beings. Rituals like 'Ka Shad Kynthei' (ritual of sowing) and 'Ka Pom Blai' (ritual of the first fruits) are performed to honor the earth and seek blessings for agricultural abundance.

In essence, the Khasi tribe's unique matrilineal society, vibrant festivals, and reverence for nature are integral to their cultural identity and way of life. Through their customs, rituals, and spiritual practices, the Khasis continue to uphold their deep-rooted connection to the environment and preserve their cultural heritage for future generations.

The Mizo tribes of Mizoram, renowned for their skilled craftsmanship and vibrant cultural heritage, have made significant contributions to India's artistic landscape, particularly in bamboo and cane work. Their traditional houses, constructed with locally sourced materials and adorned with intricate carvings and designs, serve as architectural marvels that reflect their artistic ingenuity and cultural pride.

Bamboo and cane work is integral to Mizo craftsmanship, with artisans meticulously weaving, carving, and shaping these versatile materials into a wide range of products, including baskets, mats, furniture, musical instruments, and decorative items. The intricate patterns and designs adorning these creations are often inspired by Mizo folklore, myths, and motifs from nature, showcasing the tribe's deep connection to their surroundings and cultural heritage.

Mizo festivals, such as Chapchar Kut and Mim Kut, provide vibrant expressions of the tribe's cultural identity and traditions. Chapchar Kut, celebrated with great enthusiasm during the spring season, marks the clearing of the hill slopes for jhum cultivation (slash-and-burn agriculture) and is accompanied by traditional dances, songs, and rituals that express gratitude for a successful harvest. Mim Kut, on the other hand, is a post-harvest festival celebrated with similar fervor, featuring festivities that celebrate the abundance of nature and communal harmony.

Traditional Mizo dances, like the Cheraw (bamboo dance) and Chheih Lam (community dance), are integral parts of these festivals, symbolizing unity, joy, and cultural pride. The rhythmic movements of dancers weaving in and out of bamboo poles in the Cheraw dance, accompanied by traditional music and songs, showcase the tribe's agility, coordination, and artistic flair. Similarly, the Chheih Lam dance, performed in a circular formation, embodies the spirit of community bonding and collective celebration.

The Rituals and ceremonies associated with Mizo festivals often reflect the tribe's spiritual beliefs and reverence for nature. Offerings of traditional dishes and locally brewed rice beer are made to ancestral spirits and deities, seeking their blessings for prosperity, fertility, and well-being. These rituals, passed down through generations, reinforce cultural values, strengthen social bonds, and foster a sense of belonging within the community.

In essence, the Mizo tribes of Mizoram exemplify a rich cultural heritage rooted in skilled craftsmanship, vibrant festivals, and a deep reverence for nature. Through their artistic expressions, rituals, and communal celebrations, the Mizo people continue to uphold their cultural identity and preserve their unique traditions for future generations to cherish and admire.

The Bodo tribes, spanning across Assam, parts of West Bengal, and Meghalaya, boast a vibrant cultural heritage deeply rooted in agriculture, weaving, and traditional crafts. Their rich traditions, rituals, and festivals serve as testaments to their deep connection to the land, strong community ties, and artistic ingenuity.

Agriculture forms the backbone of Bodo society, with traditional farming practices such as rice cultivation, horticulture, and animal husbandry being integral to their way of life. Bodo farmers are known for their skillful techniques in terraced farming, which optimize land use and ensure sustainable agricultural practices. The cycle of sowing, harvesting, and celebrating the bounty of nature is central to Bodo culture, with festivals like Bwisagu and Baishagu serving as joyous occasions to express gratitude to the deities for a successful harvest.

Bwisagu and Baishagu are vibrant festivals that bring together Bodo communities in celebration and camaraderie. These festivals, marked by colourful dances, melodious music, and elaborate feasts, reflect the tribe's cultural vibrancy and social cohesion. Traditional dances like Bagurumba, Bardwisikhla, and Baisago highlight the tribe's artistic prowess and storytelling traditions, depicting themes of nature, love, and community life.

The Bodos' reverence for nature is evident in their rituals, customs, and everyday practices. Sacred groves, rivers, and hills are revered as abodes of deities and spirits, with rituals and offerings made to seek their blessings for prosperity and well-being. Traditional crafts such as handloom weaving, pottery, and bamboo and cane work also reflect the tribe's intimate relationship with nature, with artisans drawing inspiration from their surroundings to create intricate designs and motifs.

Social cohesion and community solidarity are hallmarks of Bodo society, with a strong emphasis on collective welfare and mutual support. Village councils, comprising respected elders and leaders, play a crucial role in governance, dispute resolution, and preserving cultural traditions. Festivals, weddings, and other social gatherings serve as opportunities for strengthening these communal ties, with rituals, songs, and dances fostering a sense of belonging and identity among Bodo tribes.

The Bodo tribes of Assam and neighboring regions epitomize a rich cultural heritage rooted in agriculture, weaving, and traditional crafts. Their festivals, rituals, and artistic expressions not only celebrate their cultural identity but also reflect their deep reverence for nature and their strong sense of community. Through their traditions and customs, the Bodos continue to uphold their cultural legacy and pass down their rich heritage to future generations.

The tribal cultures of Odisha and North-East India stand as vibrant tapestries, woven with threads of tradition, spirituality, and resilience. Spanning across diverse landscapes and ethnic groups, these indigenous communities have upheld their rich heritage through centuries, fostering a profound connection to their land, customs, and ancestral wisdom.

In Odisha, the state's tribal communities, including the Kondh, Santal, and Gond tribes, have preserved their cultural identity through vibrant festivals, intricate crafts, and spiritual rituals. Festivals like the Kondh Kui festival and Santal Sohrai are occasions for communal celebration, where traditional dances, music, and rituals bring together families and communities in joyous harmony. These festivals not only honor the cycles of nature but also reinforce social bonds and cultural pride.

Similarly, in North-East India, the mosaic of tribal cultures in states like Nagaland, Manipur, Mizoram, and Meghalaya offers a kaleidoscope of traditions and customs. The Hornbill Festival in Nagaland, for instance, is a grand celebration of Naga culture, featuring traditional dances, music, and crafts that showcase the tribe's vibrant cultural heritage. In Mizoram, the Mizo tribes' intricate bamboo and cane work reflect their artistic ingenuity and deep connection to nature, while festivals like Chapchar Kut and Mim Kut embody the spirit of community, gratitude, and renewal.

At the heart of these tribal cultures lies a profound reverence for nature and the spiritual world. Sacred groves, rivers, and mountains are revered as manifestations of divine spirits, with rituals and ceremonies conducted to seek blessings for prosperity and well-being. Traditional crafts, such as weaving, pottery, and woodcarving, often draw inspiration from the natural world, with motifs and designs reflecting the tribes' intimate relationship with their environment.

Despite the challenges of modernization and social change, these tribal communities continue to embrace and celebrate their cultural identity with resilience and pride. Through their enduring traditions, strong sense of community, and reverence for nature, they offer a glimpse into a way of life that is deeply rooted in tradition, spirituality, and harmony with the natural world. As custodians of India's indigenous heritage, they enrich the cultural tapestry of the nation, reminding us of the importance of preserving and honoring our diverse cultural legacy for generations to come.

CHAPTER XI

Unity in Diversity

India's "Unity in Diversity" is a testament to the country's ability to weave together a rich mosaic of cultures, traditions, and identities into a cohesive national fabric. Despite its vastness and diversity, India has embraced pluralism as a foundational principle, fostering an environment where people of different backgrounds coexist harmoniously and celebrate their differences.

At the heart of India's unity lies its cultural tapestry, woven with threads of traditions, customs, and rituals that reflect the country's multifaceted heritage. From the colourful festivals of Diwali, Eid, Holi, and Christmas to the diverse cuisines, music, and art forms, India's cultural landscape is as varied and vibrant as its people. These cultural expressions serve as bridges that connect communities across linguistic, religious, and regional divides, fostering a sense of belonging and mutual respect.

India's linguistic diversity is another hallmark of its unity in diversity. With over 22 officially recognized languages and hundreds of dialects spoken across the country, language serves as a powerful symbol of identity and heritage. Despite the linguistic diversity, Indians have developed a remarkable ability to communicate and interact across language barriers, transcending linguistic differences to forge bonds of friendship and solidarity.

Religious pluralism is deeply ingrained in India's social fabric, with Hinduism, Islam, Christianity, Sikhism, Buddhism, and Jainism coexisting peacefully for centuries. India's secular constitution guarantees freedom of religion and ensures that all citizens have the right to practice their faith without fear of discrimination or persecution. This ethos of religious tolerance has fostered a spirit of communal harmony and mutual respect among India's diverse religious communities.

Moreover, India's unity in diversity finds expression in its democratic institutions and principles. With a robust democratic framework, India provides a platform for people from all walks of life to participate in the decision-making process and contribute to the nation's progress. Through free and fair elections, vibrant civil society, and a robust judiciary, India upholds the values of equality, liberty, and fraternity, ensuring that all citizens are treated with dignity and respect.

Despite the challenges posed by social, economic, and political differences, India's unity in diversity remains a source of strength and resilience. Through dialogue, inclusivity, and equitable development policies, India continues to nurture its pluralistic heritage and promote harmony among its diverse communities. As a shining example of multiculturalism and coexistence, India inspires nations around the world to embrace the richness of their own cultural tapestries and celebrate the beauty of diversity.

India's commitment to inclusivity and tolerance serves as the cornerstone of its unity in diversity, fostering an environment where people of different backgrounds can coexist harmoniously and thrive together. This ethos permeates every aspect of Indian life, shaping its vibrant festivals, rich traditions, democratic principles, and constitutional values.

In the realm of festivals and traditions, India showcases its commitment to inclusivity through celebrations that transcend religious, regional, and cultural boundaries. Festivals like Diwali, Eid, Christmas, and Holi are celebrated with equal fervor and enthusiasm by people of all faiths and backgrounds. These celebrations serve as occasions for communal bonding, cross-cultural exchange, and mutual respect, fostering a sense of unity and solidarity among diverse communities.

Moreover, India's commitment to inclusivity is reflected in its democratic principles and constitutional values, which uphold the rights and freedoms of all citizens regardless of their background or beliefs. India's secular constitution guarantees freedom of religion, speech, and expression, ensuring that all individuals have the right to practice their faith and express their opinions without fear of discrimination or persecution. This commitment to pluralism and tolerance is enshrined in the preamble of the Indian Constitution, which declares India to be a "sovereign, socialist, secular, democratic republic" committed to ensuring justice, liberty, equality, and fraternity for all its citizens.

Furthermore, India's commitment to inclusivity is evident in its efforts to promote social cohesion and harmony through affirmative action policies, educational initiatives, and community development programs. The government has implemented various measures to empower marginalized communities, promote gender equality, and foster interfaith dialogue and understanding. These initiatives aim to bridge social and economic disparities, promote social justice, and create a more inclusive and equitable society where every individual has the opportunity to fulfill their potential and contribute to the nation's progress.

In essence, India's commitment to inclusivity and tolerance lies at the heart of its unity in diversity, serving as a guiding principle that promotes mutual respect, understanding, and cooperation among its diverse population. By embracing its rich tapestry of cultures, traditions, and beliefs, India continues to uphold its pluralistic heritage and strengthen the bonds of unity that unite its people across differences. As a beacon of multiculturalism and coexistence, India sets an example for the world, demonstrating the transformative power of inclusivity and tolerance in building a more peaceful, prosperous, and harmonious society.

India's festivals are vibrant expressions of its rich cultural diversity, serving as kaleidoscopes of colours, traditions, and celebrations that unite people from diverse backgrounds in a spirit of joy and camaraderie. These festivals, spanning religious, regional, and cultural spectrums, are not just occasions for merriment but also opportunities for communal bonding, cross-cultural exchange, and the celebration of shared humanity.

Diwali, known as the Festival of Lights, is celebrated by Hindus, Sikhs, Jains, and Buddhists across India and around the world. The festival signifies the triumph of light over darkness, good over evil, and knowledge over ignorance. During Diwali, homes and streets are adorned with diyas (earthen lamps) and colourful decorations, symbolizing the victory of light over darkness. Families come together to exchange sweets, gifts, and good wishes, while communities organize fireworks displays, music, and dance performances to celebrate the festive spirit.

Eid ul-Fitr and Eid ul-Adha are celebrated by Muslims across India with great enthusiasm and fervor. Eid ul-Fitr marks the end of Ramadan, the month of fasting, and is a time for prayers, feasting, and sharing with family and friends. Eid ul-Adha, also known as the Festival of Sacrifice, commemorates the willingness of Prophet Ibrahim to sacrifice his son as an act of obedience to God. Muslims gather for prayers, exchange gifts, and distribute meat to the needy, emphasizing the values of charity, compassion, and community solidarity.

Christmas, celebrated by Christians across India, is a time of joy, peace, and goodwill. Churches are decorated with lights, candles, and Christmas trees, while carols and hymns fill the air with festive cheer. Families gather for midnight mass, exchange gifts, and enjoy sumptuous feasts, celebrating the birth of Jesus Christ and the message of love and redemption that he embodies.

Holi, known as the Festival of colours, is celebrated with exuberance and playfulness across India. People of all ages gather to smear each other with coloured powders and spray water, symbolizing the arrival of spring and the victory of good over evil. Holi transcends barriers of caste, creed, and gender, bringing people together in a riot of colours and laughter, fostering a sense of unity and camaraderie.

Durga Puja, celebrated predominantly in West Bengal, is a grand celebration of the goddess Durga's victory over the demon Mahishasura. Elaborately crafted pandals (temporary temples) are erected, showcasing intricate sculptures of the goddess and her divine entourage. Families visit pandals to offer prayers, witness cultural performances, and partake in festive meals, uniting in devotion and celebration of the divine feminine.

India's festivals are vibrant reflections of its cultural mosaic, embodying the spirit of inclusivity, tolerance, and unity in diversity. Through these celebrations, people from diverse backgrounds come together to share in each other's joy, forge bonds of friendship, and celebrate the rich tapestry of traditions that make India truly unique.

India's linguistic diversity is a hallmark of its cultural richness and complexity, reflecting centuries of migration, trade, and cultural exchange. With over 22 officially recognized languages and thousands of dialects spoken across the length and breadth of the country, India stands as a testament to the power of language to shape identity and preserve heritage.

The linguistic landscape of India is incredibly diverse, with each language representing a unique window into the history, culture, and traditions of its speakers. From Hindi and Bengali to Tamil and Telugu, India's languages encompass a wide range of linguistic families, including Indo-European, Dravidian, and Austroasiatic, each with its own distinct grammar, vocabulary, and script.

Despite the linguistic plurality, Indians have developed a remarkable ability to communicate and interact across linguistic boundaries, fostering a sense of national unity and identity that transcends linguistic differences. Multilingualism is a way of life in India, with many individuals proficient in multiple languages and dialects, allowing for seamless communication and cultural exchange across diverse communities.

This linguistic diversity is not just a reflection of India's past but also a driving force for its future. India's linguistic diversity is celebrated and protected by the Constitution, which recognizes the importance of preserving and promoting linguistic heritage as a fundamental aspect of cultural identity. Through initiatives such as the preservation of indigenous languages, the promotion of multilingual education, and the development of language technology, India strives to ensure that all its citizens have the opportunity to learn, use, and preserve their mother tongue.

Moreover, India's linguistic diversity serves as a source of cultural pride and unity, with languages serving as powerful symbols of identity and belonging. Language is deeply intertwined with cultural practices, rituals, and traditions, shaping the way individuals perceive themselves and interact with the world around them. By embracing linguistic diversity and fostering a culture of multilingualism, India not only strengthens its social cohesion but also enriches its cultural landscape, ensuring that the voices and stories of its diverse communities are heard and valued.

In essence, India's linguistic diversity is a testament to the country's rich tapestry of cultures, traditions, and identities. By recognizing and celebrating the linguistic heritage of its people, India fosters a sense of unity, pride, and belonging that transcends geographical and cultural boundaries, reaffirming its commitment to inclusivity, diversity, and pluralism.

Religious diversity is another hallmark of India's pluralistic heritage, with Hinduism, Islam, Christianity, Sikhism, Buddhism, and Jainism among the major religions practiced in the country. The coexistence of multiple faiths has not only enriched India's cultural landscape but also fostered a spirit of religious tolerance and mutual respect. India's secular constitution guarantees freedom of religion, ensuring that all citizens have the right to practice their faith without fear of discrimination or persecution.

India's unity in diversity is also enshrined in its democratic ethos and commitment to social justice. The principles of equality, liberty, and fraternity, as enshrined in the Indian Constitution, serve as the bedrock of India's pluralistic society. Through democratic institutions and mechanisms, India has sought to accommodate the diverse aspirations and interests of its people, fostering a sense of belonging and empowerment among all citizens.

Despite the challenges posed by social, economic, and political divisions, India's unity in diversity remains a source of strength and resilience. Through dialogue, reconciliation, and inclusive development initiatives, India continues to uphold its pluralistic heritage and promote harmony among its diverse communities. As a beacon of multiculturalism and coexistence, India serves as a shining example of how unity can thrive amidst diversity, inspiring nations around the world to embrace the richness of their own cultural tapestries.

CHAPTER XII

Innovations and Contributions: Science and Technology in India

India's legacy in science and technology is as ancient as it is profound, with contributions spanning centuries. From pioneering mathematical concepts to groundbreaking astronomical theories, India's intellectual heritage has left an indelible mark on the world's scientific understanding.

In the annals of history, India's mathematicians laid the groundwork for modern numerical systems. The revolutionary concept of zero, articulated by Brahmagupta in the 7th century, reshaped mathematical thinking and paved the way for complex calculations. This concept, along with the development of the decimal system, was a testament to India's mathematical ingenuity.

The advent of the decimal system, with its concept of zero as a placeholder, stands as one of the most revolutionary contributions of ancient India to the field of mathematics. Brahmagupta's elucidation of zero in the 7th century CE was a watershed moment, transforming mathematical thinking and enabling the development of sophisticated numerical systems. The decimal system, which later spread to the Arab world and Europe, facilitated complex calculations and laid the groundwork for modern arithmetic.

In tandem with advancements in mathematics, Indian astronomers made significant strides in understanding celestial phenomena. Aryabhata, a luminary of ancient Indian astronomy, proposed a heliocentric model of the solar system as early as the 5th century CE, positing that the Earth revolves around the Sun. This heliocentric theory, which predated Copernicus by over a millennium, showcased India's early grasp of astronomical principles and its commitment to empirical observation.

Moreover, Indian scholars developed sophisticated methodologies for scientific inquiry, emphasizing empirical observation and systematic analysis. The renowned astronomer Varahamihira, for instance, compiled vast astronomical data and formulated predictive models for eclipses and planetary movements. This empirical approach to scientific inquiry laid the groundwork for future advancements in astronomy and provided a template for systematic observation and analysis.

The intellectual legacy of ancient Indian science and mathematics extends far beyond its historical context, shaping the trajectory of scientific inquiry and technological innovation across the globe. The concept of zero and the decimal system, fundamental to modern mathematics, are testaments to India's enduring legacy in intellectual thought. Similarly, Aryabhata's heliocentric theory foreshadowed later astronomical revolutions, underscoring India's role as a crucible of scientific discovery.

India's ancient contributions to science and technology have left an indelible mark on human civilization, influencing the course of intellectual inquiry and technological advancement. From mathematical innovations to astronomical theories, India's intellectual heritage continues to inspire awe and reverence, underscoring the timeless relevance of its scientific achievements.

Ancient Mathematics

Aryabhata, a luminary in the field of mathematics and astronomy, introduced a range of algebraic principles and trigonometric functions in his seminal work, "Aryabhatiya," written in 499 CE. This text is divided into four sections: the Gitikapada (dealing with cosmology and the calculation of time), the Ganitapada (dealing with mathematics), the Kalakriyapada (dealing with time and its measurement), and the Golapada (dealing with the sphere and astronomy).

In the Ganitapada section, Aryabhata laid down the foundations of algebra. He introduced methods for solving linear and quadratic equations, an area of mathematics that would not be developed in Europe until centuries later. His approach to algebra involved simplifying complex problems into manageable parts, demonstrating an advanced understanding of numerical relationships and manipulation.

Aryabhata also made significant contributions to trigonometry. He was among the first to describe the sine function, calling it "ardha-jya," which means half-chord. His work included the creation of a sine table, with values calculated at intervals of 3.75 degrees, an unprecedented level of precision for the time. This table was critical for astronomical calculations and influenced later developments in trigonometry both in the Islamic world and in Europe.

In addition to algebra and trigonometry, Aryabhata made advancements in arithmetic. He discussed the properties of numbers, including rules for summing series of squares and cubes, which are essential for more advanced mathematical calculations. His method for calculating the value of pi to four decimal places (3.1416) was remarkably accurate, showcasing his profound understanding of geometry.

Aryabhata's contributions were not limited to pure mathematics. His work in astronomy, particularly in the Golapada section, included the revolutionary idea that the Earth rotates on its axis, a concept that was not widely accepted in the West until the Renaissance. He also calculated the sidereal rotation (the period it takes for the Earth to rotate once relative to the fixed stars) and the length of the solar year with remarkable accuracy.

The "Aryabhatiya" also tackled the problem of calculating the positions of planets and their orbits, demonstrating Aryabhata's deep knowledge of both theoretical and observational astronomy. His geocentric model of the solar system, where planets move in elliptical orbits, was a significant step toward understanding celestial mechanics.

Aryabhata's influence extended far beyond his lifetime. His work laid the foundation for future mathematical and astronomical endeavors in India and the broader scientific community. Scholars in the Islamic world translated and built upon his work during the Middle Ages, which later found its way into Europe during the Renaissance, significantly impacting the development of modern mathematics and science.

Aryabhata's "Aryabhatiya" was a groundbreaking work that showcased advanced understanding and innovation in algebra, trigonometry, arithmetic, and astronomy. His contributions provided a significant leap forward in mathematical thought and laid crucial groundwork for future generations of scientists and mathematicians.

Astronomy and Cosmology

In the realm of astronomy, India's ancient scholars demonstrated a profound understanding of celestial phenomena, significantly advancing the field with their observations and theories. Aryabhata, one of the most prominent astronomers and mathematicians of ancient India, proposed a revolutionary heliocentric model of the solar system in the 5ᵗʰ century CE. This model suggested that the Earth rotates on its axis and revolves around the Sun, challenging the prevailing geocentric beliefs that placed the Earth at the center of the universe. Aryabhata's insights predated Copernicus by more than a millennium, highlighting the advanced astronomical knowledge in ancient India and foreshadowing later astronomical revolutions.

Aryabhata's contributions extended beyond theoretical models. He made precise calculations of the length of the solar year and the sidereal day, which were remarkably accurate for his time. His work on the lunar and solar eclipses, where he provided detailed explanations and methods to predict these events, showcased his deep understanding of the dynamics between the Earth, the Sun, and the Moon. Aryabhata's innovative use of trigonometry in his astronomical calculations set the stage for future advancements in both mathematics and astronomy.

In addition to Aryabhata, other Indian astronomers made significant contributions to the understanding of celestial events. For instance, Varahamihira, another notable figure from the 6ᵗʰ century, compiled extensive astronomical data and created comprehensive texts like the "Brihat Samhita." His work included methods for predicting weather patterns and celestial events, demonstrating a sophisticated level of observational science. These ancient scholars developed intricate calendar systems based on their astronomical observations, enabling accurate timekeeping and the scheduling of religious and agricultural activities.

During the medieval period, India's scientific prowess continued to flourish, particularly in the field of medicine. Sushruta, often revered as the father of surgery, authored the "Sushruta Samhita," an extensive compendium of surgical techniques and medical knowledge. This text, dating back to the 6th century BCE, includes descriptions of various surgical procedures, from cataract surgery to complex reconstructive surgeries. Sushruta's work emphasized the importance of anatomy and detailed various surgical instruments and methods of sterilization, showcasing an advanced understanding of surgical practices that were far ahead of his time.

Sushruta's contributions were complemented by those of Charaka, another seminal figure in ancient Indian medicine. Charaka authored the "Charaka Samhita," one of the foundational texts of Ayurveda, India's ancient system of medicine. This text, believed to have been composed around the 2nd century BCE, focuses on internal medicine and provides detailed descriptions of the diagnosis and treatment of various diseases. Charaka's work emphasizes the importance of balancing the body's three doshas (vata, pitta, and kapha) for maintaining health and preventing illness. His holistic approach to medicine, which includes diet, lifestyle, and herbal remedies, laid the foundations for Ayurvedic practices that are still in use today.

The "Charaka Samhita" also introduced the concepts of genetics and immunity. Charaka discussed how hereditary factors influence an individual's health and traits, and he recognized the body's natural ability to resist and overcome diseases. This early understanding of genetics and immunity underscores the advanced level of medical knowledge in ancient India.

Together, the contributions of Sushruta and Charaka laid the groundwork for a comprehensive medical system that integrated surgical techniques, internal medicine, and holistic health practices. Their works were not only influential in India but also reached other parts of the world through translations and the spread of knowledge along trade routes. The principles and practices described in the "Sushruta Samhita" and the "Charaka Samhita" have endured for centuries, continuing to inform modern medical practices and holistic health approaches.

India's ancient and medieval periods were marked by remarkable advancements in astronomy and medicine. Scholars like Aryabhata, Sushruta, and Charaka pushed the boundaries of their respective fields, laying the foundations for future scientific and medical discoveries. Their work exemplifies the rich intellectual heritage of India and its enduring impact on global knowledge and practices.

Medieval Medicine

India's scientific journey transcended antiquity, ushering in an era of modern innovations and technological breakthroughs. In the realm of mathematics and physics, luminaries like Srinivasa Ramanujan and C.V. Raman made indelible contributions. Ramanujan's insights into number theory and infinite series revolutionized mathematical thinking, while C.V. Raman's discovery of the scattering of light, known as the Raman Effect, earned him global acclaim.

Modern Innovations

The advent of information technology saw India emerge as a global powerhouse, with pioneering contributions in software development and IT services. During the late 20th and early 21st centuries, India capitalized on its burgeoning pool of highly skilled engineers and IT professionals, establishing a reputation for excellence in the technology sector. The growth of India's IT industry can be largely attributed to the vision and leadership of companies like Tata Consultancy Services (TCS), Infosys, and Wipro, which spearheaded the IT revolution and transformed the nation into a key player in the global digital economy.

Tata Consultancy Services (TCS), founded in 1968, played a pivotal role in laying the foundation for India's IT industry. As one of the world's largest IT services companies, TCS has been at the forefront of technological innovation, providing cutting-edge solutions in software development, consulting, and business process outsourcing. TCS's commitment to quality and its emphasis on research and development have propelled it to the top of the global IT services market, earning it a reputation for excellence and reliability.

Infosys, established in 1981, is another titan of India's IT industry. With its emphasis on innovation, Infosys has been instrumental in developing new technologies and processes that have revolutionized the IT services sector. The company's pioneering work in the areas of artificial intelligence, cloud computing, and digital transformation has set new standards for the industry. Infosys's global delivery model, which optimizes cost and efficiency by leveraging resources from multiple geographies, has become a benchmark for IT services worldwide.

Wipro, founded in 1945 as a vegetable oil manufacturer, transformed itself into a leading IT services company in the late 20th century. By the 1990s, Wipro had diversified into software development and IT consulting, quickly becoming a major player in the global IT market. Wipro's focus on sustainability and innovation has driven its growth and success, with the company making significant strides in emerging technologies such as blockchain, cybersecurity, and the Internet of Things (IoT). Wipro's global reach and comprehensive service offerings have established it as a trusted partner for businesses around the world.

In the realm of space exploration, the Indian Space Research Organisation (ISRO) has achieved remarkable feats, cementing India's position as a major space-faring nation. Founded in 1969, ISRO has pursued a vision of harnessing space technology for national development, executing a series of ambitious and cost-effective space missions. One of ISRO's most notable achievements is the Mars Orbiter Mission (Mangalyaan), launched in 2013. This mission marked a historic milestone as India became the first Asian country to reach Martian orbit and the first nation in the world to do so on its maiden attempt.

Mangalyaan, an acronym for Mars Orbiter Mission, demonstrated ISRO's technological prowess and innovative spirit. The mission aimed to develop the technologies required for interplanetary missions, gather scientific data on Martian surface and atmosphere, and enhance India's understanding of the Martian climate and geology. Despite operating on a budget significantly lower than similar missions by other space agencies, Mangalyaan succeeded in achieving all its objectives, showcasing India's ability to deliver high-impact space missions in a cost-effective manner.

ISRO's achievements extend beyond Mars exploration. The organisation has developed a robust space program that includes satellite launches, lunar exploration, and earth observation missions. The Chandrayaan missions, aimed at exploring the Moon, have yielded valuable scientific data and positioned India as a key player in lunar exploration. Chandrayaan-1, launched in 2008, confirmed the presence of water molecules on the Moon, a discovery that had significant implications for future lunar missions and the understanding of lunar geology.

ISRO's success is built on its innovative approach and emphasis on indigenous development. The organisation has developed a range of launch vehicles, such as the Polar Satellite Launch Vehicle (PSLV) and the Geosynchronous Satellite Launch Vehicle (GSLV), which have proven to be reliable and versatile platforms for launching satellites into various orbits. ISRO's ability to consistently deliver successful missions has fostered international collaborations and commercial partnerships, further enhancing India's reputation in the global space community.

In conclusion, India's emergence as a global powerhouse in information technology and space exploration is a testament to its innovative spirit, technical expertise, and strategic vision. The contributions of companies like TCS, Infosys, and Wipro have transformed the IT landscape, driving economic growth and positioning India as a leader in the digital age. Meanwhile, ISRO's remarkable achievements in space exploration have demonstrated India's technological capabilities and established it as a key player in the global space arena. Together, these advancements underscore India's potential to shape the future of technology and exploration on a global scale.

Space Exploration and Information Technology

Throughout history, India has been home to a pantheon of scientific luminaries whose contributions have significantly shaped the course of human knowledge. These visionaries, from ancient mathematicians like Aryabhata to modern-day innovators like Srinivasa Ramanujan and the scientists of the Indian Space Research Organisation

(ISRO), have made enduring contributions that continue to inspire generations of thinkers and innovators worldwide.

Aryabhata, one of the earliest and most notable figures in Indian mathematics and astronomy, laid the foundations for many future advancements. His work, "Aryabhatiya," composed in 499 CE, introduced revolutionary concepts in mathematics and astronomy, including the value of pi, the concept of zero, and the heliocentric model of the solar system. Aryabhata's pioneering work demonstrated an advanced understanding of numerical relationships and celestial mechanics that influenced both his contemporaries and future generations.

In the modern era, Srinivasa Ramanujan emerged as a towering figure in mathematics. Despite limited formal education, Ramanujan made groundbreaking contributions to number theory, infinite series, and continued fractions. His collaboration with British mathematician G.H. Hardy at the University of Cambridge resulted in significant discoveries that have since become fundamental to modern mathematics. Ramanujan's work continues to be celebrated for its originality and depth, inspiring mathematicians around the world to explore new frontiers in mathematical theory.

The legacy of Indian innovation extends into the realm of space exploration, where ISRO has achieved remarkable feats. Founded in 1969, ISRO has propelled India into the elite league of space-faring nations through a series of ambitious and successful missions. One of ISRO's most notable achievements is the Mars Orbiter Mission (Mangalyaan), launched in 2013. This mission made India the first country to reach Mars on its maiden attempt and the fourth space agency globally to achieve this feat. Mangalyaan provided valuable scientific data about the

Martian surface and atmosphere and showcased India's ability to execute complex space missions with remarkable cost-efficiency.

ISRO's success is not limited to Mars exploration. The Chandrayaan missions, aimed at exploring the Moon, have yielded significant scientific discoveries and positioned India as a key player in lunar exploration. Chandrayaan-1, launched in 2008, confirmed the presence of water molecules on the Moon, a finding that had profound implications for future lunar missions and the understanding of lunar geology. The follow-up mission, Chandrayaan-2, aimed to further explore the Moon's south pole region, demonstrating India's commitment to advancing lunar science.

In addition to its achievements in space exploration, India has emerged as a global powerhouse in information technology. The country's IT sector, driven by companies like Tata Consultancy Services (TCS), Infosys, and Wipro, has transformed the global digital landscape. These companies have pioneered advancements in software development, IT services, and digital transformation, establishing India as a leader in the global technology industry. TCS, Infosys, and Wipro have not only contributed to economic growth but also set new standards for innovation and efficiency in the IT sector.

TCS, founded in 1968, has become one of the world's largest IT services companies, providing cutting-edge solutions in software development, consulting, and business process outsourcing. Infosys, established in 1981, has been at the forefront of technological innovation, particularly in areas like artificial intelligence, cloud computing, and digital transformation. Wipro, with its focus on sustainability and emerging technologies, has made significant strides in areas such as blockchain, cybersecurity, and the Internet of Things (IoT).

These IT giants have played a crucial role in positioning India as a global leader in the digital age. Their contributions have driven economic growth, created millions of jobs, and fostered a culture of innovation that continues to propel the industry forward. The success of India's IT sector is a testament to the nation's ability to harness its intellectual capital and adapt to the rapidly evolving technological landscape.

In conclusion, India's journey in science and technology is a testament to human ingenuity and perseverance. From ancient mathematical treatises to cutting-edge space missions, India's contributions stand as a testament to the enduring spirit of exploration and discovery that transcends time and space. The nation's scientific and technological achievements have not only advanced human knowledge but also inspired countless individuals to pursue new frontiers in their respective fields. As India continues to innovate and push the boundaries of what is possible, its legacy of excellence in science and technology will undoubtedly continue to inspire future generations worldwide.

India's rich legacy in science and technology spans from ancient times to the modern era, marked by groundbreaking contributions in mathematics, astronomy, medicine, information technology, and space exploration. Ancient scholars like Aryabhata and Sushruta laid the foundations for mathematics and surgery, respectively, while modern luminaries such as Srinivasa Ramanujan and the scientists of ISRO have propelled India to the forefront of global innovation. The pioneering work of IT giants like TCS, Infosys, and Wipro has established India as a leader in the digital age. Collectively, these achievements reflect India's enduring spirit of exploration and discovery, continuing to inspire and shape the future of global science and technology.

CHAPTER XIII

Preserving India's Cultural Heritage

India's cultural heritage is a kaleidoscope of traditions, beliefs, and practices that have been passed down through generations, shaping the identity of the nation and its people. From the ancient civilizations of the Indus Valley to the medieval kingdoms of the Deccan, India's rich tapestry of cultural diversity reflects the myriad influences of history, religion, language, and geography. Yet, in the face of rapid urbanization, industrialization, and globalization, this heritage is under threat, as ancient monuments crumble, traditional crafts languish, and indigenous languages fade into obscurity.

As custodians of India's cultural legacy, we are tasked with the formidable challenge of preserving and protecting these invaluable treasures for future generations. This responsibility requires us to navigate a complex landscape of competing interests, balancing the imperatives of economic development and progress with the imperative of heritage conservation and cultural preservation. It requires us to find innovative solutions to the myriad challenges facing India's cultural heritage, from urban encroachment and environmental degradation to political instability and social upheaval.

At the heart of this endeavor lies a deep commitment to honoring and celebrating India's diverse traditions, recognizing the inherent value of cultural heritage as a source of identity, pride, and belonging. It requires us to foster a sense of stewardship and ownership among communities, empowering them to take an active role in the preservation and promotion of their cultural heritage. It requires us to invest in education and awareness programs that highlight the significance of India's cultural diversity and the importance of preserving it for future generations.

But perhaps most importantly, preserving India's cultural heritage requires us to embrace a holistic approach that recognizes the interconnectedness of all aspects of our cultural legacy – from ancient monuments and archaeological sites to traditional crafts, performing arts, and intangible cultural practices. It requires us to leverage the power of technology and innovation to document, digitize, and disseminate knowledge about India's cultural heritage, making it accessible to a global audience while ensuring its protection and preservation for future generations.

In the face of these challenges, we are reminded of the profound importance of India's cultural heritage as a repository of wisdom, creativity, and resilience. It is a legacy that has endured for millennia, surviving wars, invasions, and natural disasters, and it is our responsibility to ensure that it continues to thrive in the face of the challenges of the modern world. By embracing the richness and diversity of India's cultural heritage, we can create a future that is rooted in the past, yet dynamic and vibrant, celebrating the enduring legacy of India's cultural mosaic for generations to come.

The relentless march of urbanization and industrialization poses a significant threat to India's cultural heritage, as ancient monuments, archaeological sites, and traditional cultural landscapes are increasingly vulnerable to encroachment, pollution, and neglect. As cities expand and infrastructure projects proliferate, historic sites are often relegated to the periphery of urban development, overshadowed by towering skyscrapers and sprawling highways. In the race for progress, the preservation of India's cultural heritage is frequently sidelined, viewed as an impediment to economic growth rather than a vital component of national identity and pride.

Efforts to balance the demands of development with the imperative of heritage conservation are fraught with challenges. Robust legislation and regulatory frameworks are essential to protect heritage sites from indiscriminate development and encroachment. However, enforcement mechanisms are often inadequate, and legal loopholes allow for the exploitation of cultural resources for commercial gain. Furthermore, the lack of coordination between different government agencies responsible for urban planning, heritage conservation, and environmental protection exacerbates the problem, leading to fragmented approaches and ineffective outcomes.

Community engagement plays a crucial role in preserving India's cultural heritage, as local residents are often the custodians of traditional knowledge and practices passed down through generations. Empowering communities to take an active role in the preservation and management of heritage sites fosters a sense of ownership and stewardship, ensuring that cultural assets are valued and protected for future generations. Additionally, raising awareness about the importance of cultural heritage through education and outreach programs helps to cultivate a culture of respect and appreciation for India's diverse traditions and history.

Innovative approaches to heritage conservation are also essential to address the unique challenges posed by urbanization and industrialization. Adaptive reuse strategies, such as converting historic buildings into cultural centers or boutique hotels, can breathe new life into neglected heritage sites while generating revenue for their upkeep. Similarly, sustainable development practices, such as green infrastructure and eco-tourism initiatives, can mitigate the environmental impact of urban expansion while preserving the cultural integrity of surrounding landscapes.

Ultimately, the preservation of India's cultural heritage requires a multi-faceted approach that integrates urban planning, environmental stewardship, community engagement, and innovative conservation strategies. By recognizing the intrinsic value of cultural heritage as a source of identity, pride, and inspiration, and by committing to its protection and preservation, India can ensure that its rich cultural legacy endures for future generations to cherish and celebrate.

In response to these challenges, a myriad of initiatives have been undertaken to preserve India's cultural heritage and foster a deeper appreciation for its significance. Heritage conservation organizations, governmental agencies, and non-profit groups work tirelessly to restore and maintain historic sites, monuments, and architectural landmarks, employing state-of-the-art conservation techniques and technologies to ensure their longevity. Additionally, cultural education programs seek to raise awareness about India's diverse heritage among the younger generation, instilling a sense of pride and responsibility in safeguarding their cultural legacy.

Museum preservation also plays a crucial role in safeguarding India's cultural heritage, serving as repositories of art, artifacts, manuscripts, and ephemera that chronicle the nation's rich history and traditions.

Museums not only provide a platform for public engagement and education but also serve as custodians of cultural memory, preserving and interpreting India's heritage for future generations. Initiatives to modernize museum facilities, enhance exhibition design, and digitize collections have expanded access to India's cultural treasures while ensuring their long-term preservation and conservation.

Despite the challenges, there are numerous success stories and ongoing projects aimed at safeguarding India's diverse traditions for future generations. From the restoration of ancient temples and forts to the revitalization of traditional crafts and performing arts, these efforts demonstrate the resilience and determination of communities across India to preserve their cultural heritage in the face of adversity. Collaborative initiatives between government agencies, local communities, and international partners have proven instrumental in protecting and promoting India's cultural diversity, fostering a sense of pride and ownership among stakeholders.

As we navigate the complexities of preserving India's cultural heritage in the modern world, we are reminded of the imperative to balance progress with preservation, innovation with tradition, and development with conservation. By embracing a holistic approach that integrates heritage conservation, museum preservation, and cultural education, we can ensure that India's diverse traditions endure as sources of inspiration, identity, and pride for generations to come.

In conclusion, the exploration of women's roles in Indian culture reveals a complex narrative of tradition, resilience, and progress. From ancient times to the modern era, women have navigated societal expectations and barriers, contributing significantly to various fields despite facing challenges and discrimination. While historical legacies and patriarchal norms have shaped women's experiences, their achievements and

CHAPTER XIV

The Role of Women in Indian Culture

Throughout history, women in Indian culture have played multifaceted roles shaped by tradition, religion, and societal norms. From ancient times to the present day, the status and roles of women have evolved significantly, reflecting changes in political, social, and economic landscapes.

In ancient India, women occupied respected positions in society, with some even holding positions of power and influence. The Rigveda, one of the oldest Indian scriptures, acknowledges the importance of women in domestic and social spheres. However, as society became more stratified and patriarchal, women's roles became more restricted. The caste system, purdah system, and prevalent practices like child marriage and sati further limited women's autonomy and agency.

During the medieval period, women's roles continued to be influenced by religious and cultural practices. While some women enjoyed positions of authority and prominence, such as rulers, scholars, and poets, the prevailing norms often relegated women to subordinate roles within the family and society. The influence of Islamic culture, particularly in regions ruled by Muslim dynasties, introduced new norms and customs that impacted women's lives.

In modern India, significant strides have been made towards gender equality and women's empowerment, yet challenges persist. Women have made significant contributions across various fields, breaking barriers and shattering stereotypes. In politics, figures like Indira Gandhi, India's first female Prime Minister, and Pratibha Patil, the country's first female President, have demonstrated women's capabilities in leadership roles.

In the realm of literature and arts, women like Sarojini Naidu, Amrita Pritam, and Arundhati Roy have left an indelible mark, using their voices to challenge social norms and advocate for change. Their works have not only enriched Indian culture but also sparked conversations about gender, identity, and social justice.

In academia and science, women such as Kalpana Chawla, the first woman of Indian origin in space, and Sudha Murthy, a renowned author and philanthropist, have inspired generations with their achievements and contributions to knowledge and innovation.

Efforts towards women's empowerment and gender equality are underway. Legislative reforms, educational initiatives, and grassroots movements led by women's rights activists and organizations aim to address systemic inequalities and create a more inclusive society.

The role of women in Indian culture is a complex tapestry woven with tradition, resilience, and aspiration. While historical legacies and societal norms have shaped women's experiences, their contributions to various fields underscore their agency and potential. By acknowledging and addressing systemic barriers, India can harness the full potential of its women and create a more equitable and inclusive society for future generations.

About The Author

Nitesh Nirupam is an accomplished author, percussionist, and graphic designer, whose multifaceted talents and passions have shaped a diverse and dynamic life journey. Born and raised in the bustling city of Ghaziabad, Nitesh discovered their love for storytelling at a young age, finding solace and inspiration in the pages of books that transported them to far-off lands and imaginary worlds.

As they grew older, Nitesh's creative spirit found expression not only in literature but also in the rhythmic beats of percussion instruments. From the first moment they picked up a drum, they knew that music would become an integral part of their identity, allowing them to communicate emotions and stories in ways that words alone could not.

But Nitesh's talents extend beyond the realms of literature and music. With a natural gift for public speaking and a passion for debate, they have honed their persuasive abilities to engage and inspire audiences on a wide range of topics, from social justice issues to the power of storytelling in shaping our collective consciousness.

In addition to their creative pursuits, Nitesh is also a dedicated martial artist, having achieved a black belt and earned a state-level silver medal in taekwondo. Their journey in martial arts has taught them discipline, perseverance, and the importance of physical and mental strength in overcoming life's challenges.

Driven by a relentless curiosity and a thirst for new experiences, Nitesh's commitment to personal growth extends to language learning, with a particular focus on mastering German. As a certified A1 level German speaker, they embrace the opportunity to connect with people from different cultures and backgrounds, enriching their understanding of the world and expanding their horizons.

With a multitude of talents and a boundless enthusiasm for life, Nitesh Nirupam continues to push boundaries and explore the richness of life's experiences, inspiring others to embrace their passions and pursue their dreams with courage and conviction.

The Author thanks the readers for reading the book!

Bibliography

1. **ChatGPT OpenAI** | Retrieved from https://openai.com/chatgpt
2. **Wikipedia** | Retrieved from https://en.wikipedia.org
3. **Encyclopædia Britannica** | Retrieved from https://www.britannica.com
4. **Quora** | Retrieved from https://www.quora.com
5. **Indian Space Research Organisation (ISRO)** | Retrieved from https://www.isro.gov.in
6. **Google Scholar** | Retrieved from https://scholar.google.com
7. **JSTOR** | Retrieved from https://www.jstor.org
8. **IEEE Xplore** | Retrieved from https://ieeexplore.ieee.org/Xplore/home.jsp

These sources provide a comprehensive foundation for the book. No particular links have been mentioned for a specific topic as Major Information was taken from these websites.

Thank You!

Milton Keynes UK
Ingram Content Group UK Ltd.
UKHW040215091024
449407UK00005BA/18